THE CHURCH AND
SCOTTISH SOCIAL DEVELOPMENT
1780–1870

The Cunningham Lectures
given in Edinburgh,
1957

THE CHURCH
AND
SCOTTISH SOCIAL
DEVELOPMENT
1780-1870

STEWART MECHIE
M.A., D.D.

*Lecturer in Ecclesiastical History
in the University of Glasgow*

LONDON
OXFORD UNIVERSITY PRESS
GLASGOW NEW YORK
1960

Oxford University Press, Amen House, London E.C.4

GLASGOW NEW YORK TORONTO MELBOURNE WELLINGTON
BOMBAY CALCUTTA MADRAS KARACHI KUALA LUMPUR
CAPE TOWN IBADAN NAIROBI ACCRA

PRINTED IN GREAT BRITAIN

CONTENTS

FOREWORD

THIS BOOK, with the exception of the first three chapters, is based on the Cunningham Lectures delivered in New College, Edinburgh, in the autumn of 1957, and I wish to express my cordial thanks to the Trustees of the lectureship who appointed me, and to the Principal and staff of New College whose kindness made the delivery of the lectures a happy and memorable experience.

The appointment to this lectureship served to focus an interest in social development and the part of the Church therein which was aroused in my student days. Closer study has shown that events are more complex and subtle than is generally realized. The so-called Industrial Revolution has been too much the prey of thesis-mongers—economic, social, anti-ecclesiastical. Many more regional studies are needed showing what actually happened during this period. A more accurate picture of the whole development could then be built up. This book, though it does not exemplify that method of approach, may be of service by suggesting the value of it and encouraging its use. I hope that it will suggest also that the influence of the Church in that development was neither so slight nor so reactionary as is often supposed.

My obligations to published works are sufficiently evident from the numerous references throughout the book; but I should like to acknowledge help received from friends who have been carrying on research in parts of the same field and have guided me to useful sources. For such help in chapters one and seven I have to thank Mr. W. H. Marwick, M.A., Department of Economic History, the University of Edinburgh; also in chapter one, the Rev. Cornelius F. Smith, B.D., Ph.D., Crossford; in chapter eight, the Rev. Thomas R. Robertson, B.D., Kilmarnock; in chapter nine, the Rev. Donald M. McFarlan, M.A., Ph.D., Jordanhill College of Education, Glasgow; and in the paragraphs on Hugh Miller in chapter ten, the Rev. John M.

Cooke, B.D., Ph.D., Stirling. I am indebted also to the Rev. William H. Rogan, B.D., minister of Paisley Abbey, who kindly made available to me a large scrap-book, now preserved in the Abbey, in which Patrick Brewster, probably in his later years, had pasted newspaper cuttings and other material bearing on his numerous controversies.

It is a pleasure to acknowledge the expert help of my colleague, the Rev. James Mackintosh, M.A., Librarian of Trinity College, Glasgow, and of the staff of the Oxford University Press.

S. M.

Trinity College,
  Glasgow.
10 *September* 1959.

INTRODUCTION

'THE social development of modern Scotland must be among the most neglected fields of historical research.'[1] So wrote Mr. W. H. Marwick in 1949. The book which he was reviewing, *The Dawn of Scottish Social Welfare* by Professor Thomas Ferguson, helped to remedy that neglect, as also did a work published the next year, *Scottish Democracy, 1815–1840* by the late Professor Laurance J. Saunders. We still lack, however, a survey of the place of the Church in that social development: and this volume is a pioneer effort towards supplying that need.

That Scottish churchmen should have an active social concern, persistent throughout the generations, should evoke no surprise, in view of the Calvinist tradition in which they were bred. What would occasion surprise would be their lack of such concern. Nevertheless, it is not superfluous to emphasize the point, for many at the present day do not readily associate social concern with the Church in Scotland. It is less than a century ago since the State took over the education of youth which had been the Church's responsibility since the Reformation; and not many years earlier since it assumed the Church's functions concerning the care of the poor. So short is the public memory that many of our contemporaries have forgotten that the Church ever had a central place in these matters.

Moreover, it is not generally known that, while the Reformed Church in Scotland soon abandoned, in practice, its pretensions to regulate all aspects of the national life—political and economic as well as domestic and social—yet it never ceased, from time to time, to make its views known and to denounce what it took to be violations of the divine order for human life. For instance, in March 1596 we find the General Assembly drawing attention to 'the commoun corruptiouns of all Estates within this realme', and among the items listed are 'cruell oppressioun of the poore tennents' and, more specifically, 'oppressioun under pretext of law, be usurie, and be contracts against law: forestalling of mercats, and regrateing be gentlemen, burgesses, and commouns; quherby pryces of victualls is mervailously raised to the great hurt of the poor; and sicklyke be girnelling of victualls, and withhalding them from the mercats, and not threshing of them out in due tyme'.[2] Strange as some of these complaints may seem today, they were familiar enough in an age when the medieval doctrines of the just price and the restraint of usury were still much more than a pious memory. It seemed clear to the churchmen of that day, and they did not hesitate to say so in the face of powerful and interested persons, that while the price of natural products, such as grain, might be generally determined in the open market, it must be a genuinely open market. Hence there must be explicit prohibition of any obvious frustrations of an open market such as forestalling, the buying up of goods before they reached the market, and regrating, the purchase of goods in the market with the intention of selling again at an enhanced figure.

Again, in the middle of the seventeenth century we find that the Commission of the General Assembly in 1648 resolved that the Solemn League and Covenant should be renewed throughout all the congregations of the kingdom, and in that connexion it published a 'Solemn Acknowledgment of public sins and breaches of the Covenant', and, among the sins declared to have become ordinary and common, we find not only blasphemy, profanation of the Lord's Day, lying and deceit, but also economic sins—'arbitrary and uncontrolled oppression and grinding of the faces of the poor by landlords and others in place and power'.[3] That prophetic note may have been struck less frequently in the eighteenth century than in the two centuries preceding and in the two centuries following; but even then it was struck. For instance, just at the beginning of our period, and before the French Revolution had turned men's minds forcibly to such matters, we find Archibald Bruce of Whitburn, the Old Light Anti-Burgher (1746–1816) in a sermon on True Patriotism published in 1785, declaring that 'it is the indispensable duty of all the professors of religion to appear openly and actively on the side of the cause of God, and to exert themselves for the public good, especially in times of great danger and opposition'.[4] He condemns the attitude of those who 'would have it believed that

zeal and public spirit cannot be indulged without vital and practical religion suffering and dying away', and he asserts that 'that
sort of Christianity, and those devotional exercises and experiences, which exclude attention to the state of Christ's kingdom without a man, and confine it entirely to a kingdom of God
within him, must flow from another spirit than that of Christ'.[5]

Indirect testimony to the place of the Scottish Church in social
matters may be found in that social and moralistic strain which
has been characteristic of Scottish economic thought. It is very
clear in Ruskin and Carlyle, but it is not lacking in Adam Smith
himself, whose outlook was broader than the group of ideas
which the nineteenth century came to associate with his name—
freedom and competition, the division of labour and the equi-
librium of prices. Smith had more corporate and social emphases,
too, and he showed himself a true Scot, standing in the educational tradition of the Scottish Reformation, in making economics but one aspect of social policy. It was not for nothing that
the Chair he occupied in the University of Glasgow was the
Chair of Moral Philosophy.

By Adam Smith's time, however, vast changes were beginning
in Scotland which were destined in the course of a century to
render the influence of the Church in social matters peripheral
instead of central. So long, indeed, as it retained its control of
the poor-relief system and of education, the Church could not
be ignored by any citizen, not even by those who rejected its
teaching and separated themselves from its worship and fellowship. Nowadays its influence is so indirect that masses of the
population can ignore it. That change is not due simply to its loss
of control in the two spheres mentioned. That loss of control was
itself symptomatic of the fact that social developments were proceeding under independent impulses that may have owed something to the Church's past teaching but owed almost nothing to
the Church's contemporary guiding.

What, then, were the social developments which ousted the
Church from its central place? To what extent did Scottish
churchmen themselves promote these developments? To what
extent did they seek to find remedies for the evils involved in
developments which they could not withstand? These are some
of the questions upon which we shall endeavour to throw light
in the chapters that follow.

1

THE AGRARIAN
AND INDUSTRIAL REVOLUTIONS

THERE is a continuity in economic development which makes it impossible to assign exact dates to economic eras; but, with Scotland, if any single year can be said to be of economic significance, that year is 1760 when the first blast furnaces of the Carron Ironworks were lit.[1] One large industrial enterprise does not make an industrial revolution: the Carron works betokened a new industrial order still lying some way ahead; hence there is good reason to follow the historian of the Industrial Revolution in Scotland in dating that development from 1780. It was an agrarian revolution which appeared in Scotland about 1760. Some improving of estates had indeed taken place in earlier decades, but the great changes which were to alter the aspect of the countryside came afterwards.[2] It is difficult two hundred years later to imagine a Scottish agriculture which was deplorably primitive, and still more to picture a Scotland in which agriculture was the basis on which almost the whole economy of the country was built. Noteworthy, too, is the paradoxical fact that precisely during the second half of the eighteenth century, when Scottish agriculture was rapidly improving its methods and products, it was also beginning to lose its relative importance and to cease to be the predominant factor in the economic fortunes of the population.[3]

In the Lowlands the agrarian revolution became evident in improved methods, more varied crops in proper rotation, the cultivation of hitherto waste land and, in many places, a decline in population.[4] In the Highlands these processes were at work, but important also was the spread of sheep-farming into areas where the only money income had hitherto been derived from the rearing of cattle for sale at the Crieff and, later, the Falkirk Tryst.[5] Accompanying these changes there were considerable changes in the extent and distribution of the population. Despite emigration the population increased more rapidly than in the first half of the century, and there was also a rising rate of increase which continued into the first two decades of the nineteenth century. Along with these increases there went changes in the distribution of the population.

From the Highlands many families, displaced by the new farming and estate management, emigrated overseas if they had the spirit and could raise the needful funds; while others made for the coasts and were allowed to establish themselves as squatters, sometimes eking out by fishing the miserable provision raised from their crofts. Others made for the southern counties, finding employment as labourers on farms or in the towns or as hands in the new cotton mills.[6] In the Lowlands the same kind of movement took place but not to the same extent, since in the Lowlands there was not usually the dire threat of starvation to impel migration, but simply the lure of higher wages and better prospects.

Almost all the writers in the Old Statistical Account show interest in the improvements in husbandry which had been going on for a generation and many of them also express a new confidence that, though the climate of Scotland might be indifferent and the soil poor, yet prosperity might be based on the minerals beneath the surface of the land.[7] The account of the parish of Sorn waxes almost lyrical over this prospect: 'In this instance, and in many others which have not yet been sufficiently explored, the bleak moors of Caledonia, and her hills covered with blue mists will doubtless be found to contain some of her most valuable treasures.'[8] Coal had indeed been mined in a primitive way for centuries and the seventeenth century was a period of continually increasing output.[9] In the eighteenth century there was a period of comparative stagnation, though the introduction of steam engines for pumping away water from the workings led to some increase in production;[10] but since there was as yet no demand for coal for the production of iron or of power, many good seams known to exist were left untouched,[11] and others were worked only on the surface.[12] At least until the close of the Napoleonic Wars the coal and iron industries could be classed among the secondary manufactures of Scotland, and it was not until the second phase of the Industrial Revolution in Scotland, which Professor Henry Hamilton dates from about

1830, that the coal and iron resources of Central Scotland began to be exploited on a large scale, leading to a vast development of blast furnaces, ironworks, engineering and shipbuilding establishments.

The notable feature of the first phase, which the same authority dates from 1780 to 1830, was the rapid rise of the cotton industry which soon displaced the linen manufacture as the largest Scottish textile manufacture. The capitalistic system, in the sense of village operatives working in their own homes but in the employment of city merchants, was well established long before anything that could be called the Industrial Revolution; but prior to about 1780 manufacturing operations in Scotland were carried on without the aid of power. Hence the household continued to be the typical unit of production and anything in the nature of factory organization was rare.[13] The textile industry in linen or wool was to be found scattered over nearly the whole country, the reason being that those who produced the raw material frequently took a part in the subsequent manufacture.[14] As regards linen, for instance, the cultivation of a patch of lint and the processing of the fibre up to the spinning stage was a recognized part of agricultural labour.[15] Even in the cotton industry which emerged from the older linen industry, whose organization it took over, the spinning-wheel and the handloom were at first widely distributed; but it was in that industry that the change from household to factory organization and from hand to power working first appeared, and, as in England, it began with spinning and spread later to weaving. Cotton seems to have afforded better remuneration than linen or wool to all parties concerned. On the other hand it differed from them in that its raw material came entirely from abroad. Like them it could count on a considerable home market, but for prosperity it required a large export market, too; and this double dependence on foreign commerce for supplies and markets made it more liable to fluctuations.

The situation of the early spinning mills was determined by the availability of water power. The first to be established were at Penicuik in 1778 and at Rothesay in 1779;[16] but cotton spinning began on a large scale in the middle of the next decade when the famous New Lanark mills were started and also the Deanston mills on the Teith. By 1787 there were nineteen cotton factories in operation and by 1834 there were one hundred and twenty-five. Sometimes hand-weaving preceded and probably determined the establishment of a spinning factory.[17] Steam power was first applied to spinning machinery in 1792.[18] Long after cotton spinning had become a factory industry the hand-loom continued to be operated in villages where the Glasgow and Paisley dealers had their agents who gave out the material and received the product.[19] The power-loom was first tried in 1793, but it was not till after the turn of the century that it began to establish itself, and the transition in weaving from hand to power working was very gradual. By that time, however, the availability of water-power was no longer of prime importance. Coal supplies and transport were of more consequence; hence the industry tended to forsake districts like the Solway coast and to concentrate in the Clyde area.[20]

In this changing situation the social concern of Scottish churchmen may be studied from two points of view, that of one of the new captains of industry, who was himself a devout churchman and, indeed, became the leader of a small new Christian denomination, and that of the writers of the parochial surveys written about 1793 for the Old Statistical Account and in the 1830's and early 1840's for the New Statistical Account. Most of these surveys were written by the parish ministers, or were prepared on the basis of information supplied by them, and we may take it that the writers were almost without exception men who might appropriately be termed churchmen.

The boom in the cotton industry in Scotland after 1780 may be attributed to several factors. One reason doubtless was that Glasgow merchants whose trade had been brought to an end by the American war were ready for a new outlet for their capital. More important was the fact that there was also capital available through the development of the linen industry, where the manufacture of the finer quality fabrics had come into the hands of a number of master-weavers who were also yarn merchants and imported large quantities of Continental yarns to supplement the supply of homespun yarns which by 1770 had become inadequate for the demand. It was they who first substituted cotton for linen yarns, and the more enterprising of them became the pioneers of the rising cotton industry.[21] Another reason for the development at this time was the major technical advances in the

textile field which had been made in England, though it should
be noted that a number of minor inventions and improvements
were later made in the Scottish cotton industry.[22]

The career of David Dale reveals how these factors operated.
He was born at Stewarton in 1739, the son of a grocer and
general dealer, and began his career as a herd lad in his native
place. He then became a weaver at Paisley, Hamilton, and Cambuslang, and later removed to Glasgow to become clerk to a silk
mercer. About 1763 he set up as a linen merchant and yarn
dealer near Glasgow Cross with Archibald Paterson as his
moneyed partner. It is said that he got the shop for £5 a year,
and to reduce expenses let part of it to a watchmaker for half
that sum. Noticing the difficulty experienced by the weavers in
procuring yarns, he tramped the countryside buying up small
quantities of linen thread spun by the farmers' wives, and later
became an importer of Continental yarn which he gave out
to the cambric and lawn weavers whom he employed.[23] Soon
he was associated with two other partnerships, one of these
manufacturing inkle, or linen tape, so called from an early Dutch
type of loom, and the other manufacturing cloth for the print-
fields.

It was in the cotton trade, however, that Dale made his most
notable ventures. In 1783 Richard Arkwright, inventor of the
'spinning-jenny', came to Glasgow and Dale induced him to visit
the Clyde at Lanark. The result was a partnership to use Arkwright's patent and the planning of the famous cotton-spinning
mills at New Lanark on the estate of the notorious Lord Brax-
field. Operations began there in 1784: mechanics were sent to
England to be instructed in the nature of the machinery: and
the mills were opened in 1785. In the meantime, however, the
courts had decided against the validity of Arkwright's patent
and the partnership was dissolved, the business being taken over
by Dale himself. The New Lanark mills, the first large cotton-
spinning mills in Scotland, were at one time the largest in
Britain. They became famous chiefly through their association
with the theories and experiments of Robert Owen, who became
Dale's son-in-law; but Dale, too, aimed at being a benevolent
employer, and some features of Owen's system at New Lanark
were begun there while Dale was still the proprietor. The general
lines of policy in the early period must be ascribed to Dale. It

appears, however, that he took little part in the actual management and seldom visited the mills, though his family spent part of the year at a house in the village.

It was difficult in those days to get factory workers. In the Lowlands the conditions of the agricultural population were relatively good, and factories held little attraction. The local people would not work or send their children to work in the mills. Dale—and Owen after him—had thus to secure the great majority of the workers from a distance. One source was the Highlands. In 1791 Dale provided employment for two hundred intending emigrants whose ship had been driven by stress of storm into Greenock. Agents were also sent to the Highlands to get in touch with the people and tell them of the encouragements offered to families at the cotton-mills. Another source of labour needs special mention—the children. The greater part of the preparatory operations in the cotton manufacture was done by hand, and as such work—picking, teasing and the like—required dexterity of fingers rather than strength of body, large numbers of children were employed. 'Families from any quarter possessed of a good moral character, and having three children fit for work, above nine years of age, are received—supplied with a house at a moderate rent, and the women and children provided with work.'[24] Many, however, were pauper children whom the parish authorities were willing to hand over to any factory owner who would take them. Dale took them in large numbers from Edinburgh, Glasgow, and elsewhere, and Owen testifies that one of the worst features of this system was not of Dale's choosing. 'The directors of the public charities', says Owen, 'from mistaken economy would not consent to send the children under their care to cotton-mills, unless the children were received by the proprietors at the ages of six, seven and eight. And Mr. Dale was under the necessity of accepting them at those ages, or of stopping the manufactory which he had commenced.'[25]

While thus following prevailing custom in recruiting labour for his mills, Dale certainly did better by those he employed than the majority of employers of his day or of a later time. He had built the village of New Lanark as well as the mills and the people were thus housed by the firm—very ill housed by modern standards. For the parish apprentices, however, a large boarding house was provided. The hours in the mills were long—thirteen hours a day, from six in the morning till seven in the evening, with an interval of half-an-hour for breakfast and an hour for dinner, making eleven and a half hours of work. A contemporary records: 'The children, both those fit for work and those who are too young for it, have the privilege of attending the school gratis, the former in the evenings, the latter through the day. Three professed teachers are paid by Mr. Dale for this purpose, and also seven assistants who attend in the evenings, one of whom teaches writing. There is also a Sunday School at which all the masters and assistants attend.'[26] Dale took similar measures at Catrine,[27] as indeed did other mill-owners such as Gillespie of North Woodside, Glasgow[28] and Henry Monteith and Company at Blantyre;[29] but at Dunfermline the complaint was made: 'Proprietors are not sufficiently attentive to the instruction of youth and providing them with teachers.'[30] Unfortunately for the working children this education took place after the day's work, between seven and nine in the evening, upon which Owen comments: 'But this kind of instruction, when the strength of the children was exhausted, only tormented them without doing any real good—for I found that none of them understood anything they attempted to read, and many of them fell asleep during the school hours.'[31] In November 1793 the number of persons employed in the mills was 1,334 of whom 1,157 were engaged in the actual processes of cotton manufacture, and of these 145 were men, 217 were women, 376 were boys and 419 were girls. Of these 795 children no fewer than 552 were under fourteen years, while 297 ranged from six to ten. The parish apprentices housed in the boarding house numbered at that time 275, and it is on record that while their number during the preceding seven years had never been less than 80 yet, despite their long hours of work, the number of deaths among them in that period was only five.[32]

It is clear that the fault lay as much with the parish authorities who sent out the children too young as with the mill managers who imposed hours of labour that were much too long. On the other hand Dale did attend to the children's feeding, clothing, shelter, and education in a way that must be considered highly enlightened for that time. Owen himself bore witness to that: 'The benevolent proprietor spared no expense to give comfort to the poor children. The rooms provided for them were spacious, always clean and well ventilated; the food was abundant, and of the best quality; the clothes were neat and useful; a surgeon was kept in constant pay to direct how to prevent or to cure disease; and the best instructors which the country afforded were appointed to teach such branches of education as were deemed likely to be useful to children in their situation. Kind and well-disposed persons were appointed to superintend all their proceedings. Nothing, in short, at first sight seemed wanting to render it a most complete charity.'[33] Elsewhere Owen said that the boarding house for the pauper children 'was under an admirable arrangement and was a strong indication of the genuine and extensive benevolence of the revered and truly good man (the late David Dale of Glasgow) who founded these works and this village. His wishes and intentions towards you all were those of a father towards his children.'[34] Owen, however, gave up engaging any more pauper apprentices, for he saw that the system was bad. 'Many of them became dwarfs in body and mind, and some of them were deformed. Their labour through the day, and their education at night, became so irksome that numbers of them continually ran away, and almost all looked forward with impatience and anxiety to the expiration of their apprenticeship of seven, eight, and nine years, which generally expired when they were from thirteen to fifteen years old. At this period of life, unaccustomed to provide for themselves, and unacquainted with the world, they usually went to Edinburgh or Glasgow, where boys and girls were soon assailed by the innumerable temptations which all large towns present, and to which many of them fell sacrifices. Thus Mr. Dale's arrangements and kind solicitude for the comfort and happiness of these children were rendered in their ultimate effect almost nugatory. They were hired by him, and sent to be employed, and without their labour he could not support them; but, while under his care, he did all that any individual circumstanced as he was could do for his fellow-creatures. The error proceeded from the children being sent from the workhouses at an age much too young for employment; they ought to have been detained four years longer and educated; and then some of the evils which followed would have been prevented.'[35]

All in all, the mills at New Lanark were probably the best

conditioned and the most humanely run in that age, though Owen, with his enlightened ideas, found much to reform. It may be added that Dale also anticipated Owen in that, when one of the mills was burnt down in 1786, he paid the workers their wages during the period till work could be resumed. He was certainly a pioneer in appreciating the fact that the welfare of the employees is the responsibility of the employer, or ought we perhaps to say rather that he carried over a pattern of paternal relations towards his employees from the earlier pre-industrial state of society?

Dale's business ventures were varied in character, location and result. Cotton works were started in several parts of the country on the lure of water-power and cheap labour. He lost heavily in two such enterprises—those at Stanley in Perthshire and those at Spinningdale (apparently his own pun) near Dornoch on the Skibo estate. In this the then laird, Dempster of Dunnichen, was financially interested, too, as was George Macintosh, a friend of Dale and father of the inventor of the macintosh. Another scheme, intended like the Dornoch one to provide work for starving Highlanders, was the Kilmore cotton-work, near Oban, where dearth of fuel was at least temporarily a handicap.[36] For a short time Dale engaged in Turkey-red dyeing of cotton yarn at Dalmarnock, along with Macintosh and Papillon, the pioneers of the process in Scotland.[37] He also erected the cotton-spinning mill on the Clyde at Blantyre, Lanarkshire, in which David Livingstone worked as a boy.[38] He sold it to James Monteith in 1792 and incurred some censure by refusing to annul the bargain in the commercial crisis which emerged upon the outbreak of war with France. Monteith, however, weathered the storm by undertaking weaving and selling of cloth as well as spinning. Dale also founded the factory at Catrine, Ayrshire, which has survived to our own day. Here, too, he was in partnership with the local laird, Alexander of Ballochmyle, for in this early industrial development in Scotland there is little, if any, evidence of that opposition between the industrial and the landed interest that has sometimes been supposed to be characteristic of the Industrial Revolution, and there is considerable evidence to the contrary. In 1801 Dale sold the Catrine works to Kirkman Finlay, son of James Finlay, founder of the firm of that name, who, like Dale, had begun as a weaver, had become a yarn merchant and then a manufacturer and exporter. Dale was partner with Sir William Douglas in a cotton mill at Kelton, Kirkcudbrightshire, which failed,[39] and he lost £20,000 in a coal-mining venture at Barrowfield. He became Glasgow agent of the Royal Bank in 1783, its business being conducted for a number of years from his own office: and till near the end of his life, after he had withdrawn from most of his business ventures, he remained a director of the Bank in Glasgow. No doubt he was able to use his banking position at times to the advantage of his other undertakings.

In all this Dale appears as a typical *entrepreneur* of the early industrial period—industrious and far-seeing, full of energy and initiative, often making large profits, but always ready to branch out into some new line of business and often making heavy losses, too. Dale used to tell his friends that three times in his life he was thrown back on the world and on each occasion could scarcely call himself worth anything.[40] His activities were manifold. 'It is impossible,' says a Glasgow writer, 'to look into our history—mercantile, manufacturing, financial, municipal, benevolent, religious—without coming on David Dale at every turn. Even distant country ministers had heard how in other parishes David Dale of Glasgow had been in those cruel times like a good providence, and sighed that he might be the *Deus ex machina* for their poor people too.'[41] As regards his civic activities it may suffice to say that he was a town councillor and twice a magistrate and that he was one of the founders and first vice-president of the Glasgow Chamber of Commerce, founded in 1783—the first in Britain.

It is probable, however, that in Dale's own eyes all his civic and business activity was subordinate to the part he took in religious and philanthropic life. If he acquired great wealth he also shared it generously with the poor. In several periods of distress during the years of scarcity at the end of the eighteenth century he chartered ships and imported grain at his own expense to sell it cheaply to the poor.[42] It was said of him, 'David Dale gives his money by shovelfuls, but God Almighty shovels it back again'. This saying is ascribed to the poor of Glasgow in a sermon on covetousness by Andrew Fuller of Kettering who got large sums from Dale when he called upon him in connexion with the Baptist Missionary Society's work in translating the

Bible into Indian languages. When the British and Foreign Bible Society was founded in 1804 Dale was so interested that he used his influence in the formation in July 1805 of the first auxiliary to the parent society, and he acted as treasurer for Glasgow and the West of Scotland.[43]

During his apprenticeship in Paisley, Dale was a member of a fellowship meeting and when he settled in Glasgow he attached himself to the College Church under the ministry of the evangelical Dr. Gillies, son-in-law of John Maclaurin. His secession from the Established Church had to do in the first instance with the question of patronage. The General Session, composed of the ministers and elders of the eight parishes into which the city was then divided, had exercised the right of patronage; but, in the middle sixties, this was challenged by the magistrates and town council. The courts decided for the latter, and they, being of the Moderate party, filled up the first vacancy, that of the Wynd Church, with a minister of that party. This gave great offence, not only to the popular party in that congregation. The result was the erection of a new church in North Albion Street, which seems to have come under the superintendence of the Relief Synod. Dale was an original subscriber to the erection of this building and he voted for its first minister. In 1768, however, John Barclay, a licentiate of the Church of Scotland and afterwards leader of the Bereans, visited Glasgow and had many interviews with Dale and others. He brought them round to his own Congregational principles, and one of the group, Archibald Paterson, Dale's first partner, erected a meeting-house for them in Greyfriars' Wynd. About the same time two parish ministers, Smith of Newburn and Ferrier of Largo, also left the Church of Scotland on similar principles, and a correspondence ensued between the two groups which led to their union. Ferrier came to Glasgow and became for a time an 'elder' of the Church there along with Dale. Thus in 1769 Dale added to all his other tasks those of a Christian preacher and pastor among the Old Scots Independents, offices which he continued to hold till his death thirty-seven years later. The Old Scots Independents were never a large body. In 1813, seven years after Dale's death, they had only twelve congregations scattered over the country, with less than five hundred members in all.[44] They held independent views of church government, rejected establishments, did not

require an 'educated ministry' and followed the Glasite principle
of a plurality of elders. These views, and particularly the practice
of functions generally reserved for the trained ministry by an
'elder' like Dale who had no claims to a College education, excited the derision of the multitude and for a time the meeting-
house was subjected to petty annoyances and Dale was hooted
and jostled in the streets. He and his friends soon lived down
such opposition, but their Church had trouble over the question
of infant baptism and a large section of the members, having
embraced Baptist principles, withdrew. Dale's preaching was
instructive and scriptural and he is said to have acquired sufficient
Hebrew and Greek to study the Scriptures in the original
tongues.[45]

One discourse from Dale's preaching ministry has been preserved, and it is of interest not only as an example of his pulpit
messages, but as containing material indicative of some of the
temptations of his own career. It was delivered on 8 January
1792, taken down by a hearer, published in the *Christian Herald*
in February 1826, and reprinted as a pamphlet. The text was
St. Luke x. 42: 'But one thing is needful'. The discourse is full
of scriptural quotations. It is plain and practical and presup-
poses the theological doctrines of the authority of Christ and of
Scripture. It is also quite brief, unless indeed the reporter has
shortened it. At one point the preacher declares: 'Whatever
draws our attention from the glorious gospel, though the thing
be lawful in itself, by producing this effect it becomes sinful, yea,
though otherwise dutiful, it ceases for the present to be duty.'
He then quotes Christ's reproof to Martha, 'Thou art cumbered
about many things', and proceeds to say: 'Our minds should be
convinced that everything we do is present duty, and in the discharge of it we should aim at glorifying God, and doing good to
ourselves and others. Diligence in business is a duty; but in this,
and in all other duties, we should be "fervent in spirit, serving
the Lord"; which cannot be the case if this duty is attended to at
the expense of another more important.'

At a later stage the preacher bears his own testimony. After
quoting 'Fear God and keep His commandments, for this is the
whole duty of man', he says: 'Have you ever found all the enjoyment you expected from any wished-for object when attained?
I myself have felt the truth of this saying in some degree, and I

hesitate not to say from my own experience, that nothing is capable of giving the mind real happiness but the glorious gospel of the ever blessed God.' Again he says: 'Riches are one great object. These frequently take to themselves wings and fly away; and though they should not, yet they profit not in the day of wrath. And if these are obtained by oppressing the poor, or withholding from the needy what his wants demand from us, the consequence is awful.'[46]

Dale is described as short and corpulent, of a cheerful temperament, lively, communicative, able to make a joke and to take a joke against himself, with a good musical taste and fond of singing some of the old Scots songs in the company of private friends. Three charges against his conduct as a business man are on record in a biographical sketch of him. First: 'It must be confessed that Mr. Dale's engaging in so many concerns, and pursuing with eagerness such a variety of large business speculations, was scarcely consistent with that moderation in all things which is enjoined on the Christian.' Second, the fact that, as he confessed, he was three times almost reduced to penury, suggests that he was 'trading on too narrow a margin, too near the verge of bankruptcy, which, had it taken place, would have involved others in injury and suffering, and brought discredit on his Christian character'. Third, some people considered him guilty of rather sharp dealing in that he was wont to hold his own assistants and people with whom he did business to the letter of their contracts in circumstances where one might have expected greater generosity in a man of his benevolence.[47] On the other hand one must set against that his abounding liberality which was often bestowed so secretly that even the recipients of it did not know who their benefactor was. For instance, he helped anonymously to maintain his fellow lay-pastor, William Cleland, an operative weaver.[48] He could on occasion be generous to offenders, too, as in the case preserved in an anecdote of his banking career. A young man presented a draft for discount which Dale considered to be forged. He sent for the young man and mentioned his suspicions. Upon the culprit's acknowledging that they were correct, Dale pointed out to him the risk he had run and then destroyed the paper. Finding that it was financial difficulties that had prompted the crime he gave the offender some money and dismissed him with an admonition.[49]

For most people bred in the liberal-socialist tradition a career like that of Dale, who had been successively weaver, man of commerce, and industrial *entrepreneur*, conjures up a picture of a grim hard-faced man, relentless, tyrannical, possibly hypo-critical, intent on profit, and the accumulation of capital, in-different to squalor, poverty and the sufferings of his fellows. Such a notion gives an utterly wrong impression of Dale. Not even in appearance and temperament, much less in his conduct, does he answer to that description. While the thought of per-sonal gain was not absent from his calculations in promoting his enterprises, he was unquestionably drawn in the same direction by a desire to provide a living for the poor and distressed. As we have seen he made more than one attempt to introduce the cotton-manufacture into the Highlands and suffered considerable loss thereby. It seems to have been this aspect of his career which impressed his contemporaries. The minister of Sorn in an account of the cotton works at Catrine refers to him as 'the pat-riotic Mr. Dale of Glasgow';[50] while the writer of the account of Kilmadock, Doune, in giving a sketch of the Deanston works on the Teith which were begun by John Buchanan about the same time as New Lanark on the Clyde, goes out of his way to pay a tribute to Dale: 'the illustrious Mr. Dale of Glasgow in his attention to the government of young persons at his works is a noble example to others. . . . In fine, this gentleman may be called the benevolent father of a numerous family and a bright luminary to Scotland.'[51] It is significant, too, that the writer of the biographical sketch of Dale in the fifth volume of the *Bio-graphical Dictionary* of *Eminent Scotsmen*, published fifty years after his death, introduces him as 'this eminent philanthropist'. He had undoubtedly a social concern, and for his day it was both enlightened and practical.

It may seem strange to those who have been accustomed to think of the Industrial Revolution in terms of 'dark Satanic mills' imposed on happy country folk by a set of ruthless capitalistic adventurers, to find that contemporaries, writing in the Old Statistical Account, almost universally welcomed both the changes of their generation in agriculture and the developments in industry, since they brought increased opportunities of em-ployment and a higher standard of living. The simple fact is that these complex developments, bringing their own difficulties and drawbacks, as was apparent to some observers from the beginning, did at least deliver the people of Scotland from a fear of distress amounting at some times and in some districts to positive starvation. For that responsible people could not but rejoice. An Argyllshire minister believed that the new situation was beneficial for the country at large and even for the people concerned because 'there was scarcely any variety of wretchedness with which they were not obliged to struggle, or rather to which they were not obliged to submit'.[52] This attitude is widespread in the Old Statistical Account. With few exceptions the ministers of the parishes in Sutherland admit the primitive nature of the agriculture, and most of them comment on the absence of industries and express approval of the introduction of manufactures as well as of the granting of proper leases to improve the husbandry.[53] Significant is the use of the word patriotic with reference to any man who established a factory.[54] The minister of Old Monkland expresses himself enthusiastically and becomes almost lyrical at the thought. 'On a review of the various manufactures of this parish, how much, may we say, does the country stand indebted to the gentlemen connected with it. Let other nations adore their warriors and butchers of mankind, we will pay a just tribute of praise to those noble minds who cultivate the happy arts of industry and wealth.'[55] That such a man expected to increase his own wealth is not overlooked; but the benefit to all classes is no less emphasized— for example, 'What now gives a prospect of comfort, affluence and importance to the lower class is a spirit of cotton manufacture got in amongst us.'[56] Even by the time of the Old Statistical Account a distinct improvement in the standard of living is noted in several places, for example, Falkirk, Kilbarchan, and Glasgow.[57] The reflex action of industry on the countryside is not overlooked; for example, 'in short, these cotton works have inspired the whole country with industry and exertion for several miles around.'[58] The New Statistical Account corroborates the rise in the standard of living, sometimes giving as an instance the consumption of butcher meat. The minister of Leslie in 1836 writes: 'The manner of living has been very much altered within the last forty years. In the year 1826 there was but one butcher and he only killed a cow occasionally: now there are three who kill an ox each every week, and meet with a ready sale. . . . The improvement that has taken place in the building of the houses is very decided.'[59]

In line with such an attitude is the fact that the minister of Strathaven, writing in 1835, seems surprised and a little vexed that, despite the water-power available, no public works or mills have yet been erected in the parish.[60] Similarly the minister of Row in 1839 appears alarmed at the growing number of paupers and wishes for the introduction of 'some public works' as well as the curtailment of the facilities for dram-drinking,[61] while the minister of Dornoch a generation earlier adduces as 'an additional argument in favour of manufactures' that thereby 'the poor, at least many of them, would be made to contribute somewhat to their own support'.[62] Again, the survey of Paisley praises the man who first introduced the silk manufacture into Scotland and 'in the various branches of the manufacture gave daily bread to a thousand, frequently to fifteen hundred people'.[63]

The positive gains, then, of the new era are reckoned to be the stimulus to economic development, resulting in increased opportunities of employment, and an improved standard of living.[64] The drawbacks did not go unnoticed, but they were not reckoned so serious as we should count them now; partly, at any rate, because the new situation compared favourably with that which had so recently preceded it.

One of the worst features of early industrialism was the employment in factories of children of tender years. Reference is frequently made to this in the Statistical Accounts and the greatest satisfaction is expressed by the writers when they can report, as they do in the case of some of the largest establishments, that provision is made for the health and the education of these children. The minister of Neilston, at the time of the first survey, remarks on the 'pale and sickly' appearance of children in the cotton-mills, and forty years later a more forthright declaration is emitted from the same parish—'Indeed a radical change of system must take place throughout all the branches of the cotton trade, where at present children are employed, if ever we are to become an intellectual, moral and religious people. Government must interfere—our old religious system of education must return—children must be taught, and none permitted to enter into any of these works below the age of twelve or fourteen years, and until they have learned to read their Bible and say their catechism.'[65] In this connexion the minister of Kilsyth puts the blame on 'the poverty or shameful recklessness of the parents tempting them to apprentice the poor children at the early ages of eight, nine and ten'.[66] It ought to be added, in order to get this matter into focus, that the alternative to the factory employment of children was often home employment under no better conditions. For example, it is stated that at Balfron the children of the hand-loom weavers, as soon as they were able, were set to the loom to eke out by one or two shillings a week the pittance of the parent.[67]

What appears to us one of the most obvious abuses of early factory production was the long hours of work. A working day of eleven hours for five days a week and nine hours on Saturday was not uncommon, and, as we have seen, even children were made to work a day of ten or eleven hours.[68] Deplorable as this was, it must be set against the fact that such long hours were no new thing. Not only were they quite customary, but in some instances they were exceeded. In a depressed trade such as hand-loom weaving an Ayrshire minister in 1837 found a day of fourteen or even sixteen hours being worked in the endeavour to secure an adequate living.[69] Such long hours are particularly noted about that time in connexion with female home employment.[70]

The effects of factory employment on health were extensively noticed. As early as the first Statistical Account the fear is expressed at Neilston that 'the rapid increase of manufactures is neither friendly to the health nor morals of the people', and force is given to this statement when it is pointed out that in the cotton mills there are minute particles of cotton in the air.[71] Later at Kinnettles there is reference to 'flaxen dust inhaled',[72] while at Govan there is a comparison between the healthy appearance of the children connected with a silk factory and 'the sallow complexions of those young creatures whose unhappy destiny it is to be immured in a cotton factory'.[73] Testimony is sometimes given to the good health of factory workers, for instance at Catrine, Ballindalloch, and Dalry.[74] At Leslie it is noted that more attention is being paid to ventilation with beneficial results on the health of the workers.[75] There are frequent comparisons from the health point of view between out of door and factory employment, much to the disadvantage of the latter. At Larbert reference is made to the children of the past sent out at seven or eight to herd cattle—'a more healthful employment than that which falls to the lot of the cotton factory children of the present day, who are condemned by fate to make their first steps in this valley of tears confined all day in the unwholesome dusty air of a close room.'[76] Even on this point, however, there is something to be said on the other side. In the account of Campsie we are reminded 'that persons employed in manufactures are generally not exposed to cold and wet, the great springs of disease among the agricultural population'.[77] It is also stated at Blantyre that the ordinary food of the workers in the cotton mill is much better than that of the agricultural labourers in the neighbourhood.[78]

One aspect of the health situation, only indirectly connected with the growth of manufactures, is noted in the account of Campsie just referred to, where the minister reports that 'in the villages, especially Lennoxtown, where the inhabitants have increased in a far greater proportion than the houses, the people are too much crowded in their dwellings. The Irish labourers have imported their custom of pigging—as many persons occupying a room at night as can find space to lie in it—a practice equally inimical to health and to decency.'[79]

By the time of the Second Statistical Account the alternation of boom and slump with which the nineteenth century became all too familiar had become obvious to interested observers, and agriculture was favourably compared with industry. At Auchtertool, Fife, it is noted that 'the demand for country labour, too, scarcely ever varies, if it does not increase. But the same cannot be said of the labour of operatives in manufacturing towns.'[80]

As one might expect, however, it is the moral consequences of the new developments that bulk largely in the accounts. Some claimed that no harm seems to have resulted. For instance, the minister of Balfron in 1841 reports that 'in point of morality the mill population may bear comparison with any of the same rank in any of the parishes adjoining'.[81] Similar testimony is borne at Dalmellington, where the minister writes, 'Nothing injurious to health and morals can be charged against the employments of those engaged in manufactures . . . and the mills are not of such extent as, by the number they congregate, to seduce the minds of the young from the simplicity of rural life.'[82] Sometimes moral dangers are apprehended on the basis of experience elsewhere.

At the time of the Old Statistical Account the minister of Cathcart remarks that on the Cart there are many sites favourable for
the erection of cotton-spinning machinery, but adds that 'persons living in the neighbourhood have no great reason to wish
for their establishment as, by all accounts, they bring along with
them many causes of disturbance and many other inconveni-
ences'.[83] His successor forty years later was of a more decided
opinion, for he mentions that a cotton-mill on the Cart had been
contemplated 'but the idea of late seems to be abandoned, very
much to the gratification of the writer who has cause to con-
gratulate himself that none of the public works now existing has
been the means of introducing that sort of promiscuous and
floating population which is so apt from its irresponsible character to demoralize a neighbourhood'.[84]

It must not be supposed, however, that it was only the establishment of a factory that could give rise to a 'promiscuous and
floating population' with demoralizing accompaniments. The
minister of Maybole writing in 1837 refers to a population of
hand-loom weavers, mostly Irish, and says, 'There are no manufacturing establishments of any consequence in the parish, but,
as has invariably happened on the west coast, the influence of
Glasgow and the proximity of Ireland have drawn to the town
and every little hamlet a great population of hand-loom weavers
. . . the great proportion of the population in question are dissolute in their habits: few of them attend any place of worship. . . .'[85]

At Kilsyth surprise is expressed that with all the advantages
of the parish no great public work has been set up; but 'the consolation here is that morals might not be improved by such
erections and the consequent immigration'.[86] At Kinnettles
reference is made to the dubious moral effects of congregating
the young of both sexes in spinning-mills and manufacturing
shops,[87] while in other cases moral decline is quite definitely
suggested as a consequence of the new situation. 'As to the influence of our manufactures on morals,' says the second account
of Dundee, 'it is to be regretted that wherever multitudes of
human beings congregate, good morals are endangered', and
again, 'where multitudes are gathered together at various employments example does not always favour economy, industry
and virtue.'[88] Comparing the situation at the time of the First

Account with that in 1842 the Survey of St. Vigeans remarks that 'the dress, food and accommodation of all classes are much superior; what were foreign luxuries then have now become necessaries', but it adds: 'To be without the profession of religion was then a contemptible singularity; now it is very common, and little marked.'[89] At Greenock doubts are expressed— 'whether the increase of our manufactories by these means will add to the good morals and real happiness of the people is another and an infinitely more important question';[90] but at Dundonald the minister is quite decided and says: 'The parish, and we think happily, is still free from factories of every kind, the attempt referred to in the former account having completely failed. And as a lover of those among whom one would choose to dwell one would say, long may such attempts continue to fail! For while agriculture and the kindred arts are favourable alike to the physical and moral health, there is obviously something in such employments destructive of both.'[91] As early as the First Account the decline in morals is deplored at Glasgow: 'The strict severity and apparent sanctity of manners, formerly remarkable here, have yielded to the opposite extreme. There is now a great deal more industry on six days of the week, and a great deal more dissipation and licentiousness on the seventh. Great crimes were formerly very uncommon; but now robberies, house-breaking, swindling, pickpockets, pilferers and consequently executions are become more common.'[92]

Yet even when moral disadvantages are deplored there is no note of despair. The writer of the second survey of Falkirk was a lawyer, not a minister, but he takes a leaf out of Dr. Chalmers's book and suggests a subdivision of the parish into separate districts, each with its church and school, and remarks that 'in order that the moral improvement of the people may keep some equality with merely outward advantages an additional supply of pastoral superintendence would, humanly speaking, be very serviceable'.[93] Again, the writer of the account of Kilmadock or Doune more than forty years earlier—who was not the minister —refers to the evil consequences which followed the opening of the cotton-works on the Teith—'so many people collected in one house refined each other in all manner of wickedness. The duties of the family were neglected, the Sabbath was profaned, the instruction of Youth was forgotten, and a looseness and corruption

of manners spread, like a fatal contagion, everywhere around.'
The works, however, were taken over in 1793 by Benjamin
Flounders, a Quaker, and the account goes on to say, 'The laud-
able conduct of Mr. Flounders and the other managers of the
work has, however, wrought a very great reformation of these
abuses, and in a great measure provided remedies to the evils
mentioned above. The workmen are now sober and respectable
and the children are watched with vigilance and care.'[94]

In estimating these parish accounts one must make some
allowance for local patriotism. For example, a reader of Dr.
Scott Alison's report on the housing of the miners of Tranent[95]
would expect to find references to the matter in the contemporary
New Statistical Account for that parish, and he would be disappointed. One must conclude either that poor housing was so
common in these days that comment seemed unnecessary, or
else that local pride discreetly drew a veil over the worst features
of the parish.

The prevalent note in the Statistical Accounts is solid satisfaction with the new developments, and, though the compensat-
ing disadvantages to health and morals are not unnoticed, the
impression remains that the balance is much on the right side,
that the drawbacks are merely what one must expect in this im-
perfect world and that they must be borne until the remedies
can be found and applied. What one misses is any reference to
aspects of factory employment which soon proved irksome even
when wages were good—the impersonal discipline imposed by
the unwearying machines and the even more irritating discipline
of harsh overseers. Doubtless these were aspects which would
not readily occur to the minds of observers.

If it be asked why the writers of the accounts, concerned as
they clearly were with social conditions, did not wax indignant
more often, one would suggest three answers. A graded society
was taken for granted in those days. A man born in penury
might by native ability and good fortune attain to a competence,
to high position in the community or even to great wealth; but
that there must always be at the base of the social pyramid a
great mass of people in straitened circumstances was never
doubted. The days of famine and economic stress of the acutest
kind were so recent as to make anything superior to them
tolerated if not welcomed. Then, as we have had occasion to

3

notice with reference to the hours of labour, if the factory-worker's lot was hard, that of the home-worker might at times be even harder.

The Industrial Revolution descended upon Central Scotland with considerable rapidity, and there were many sore consequences. Nevertheless it may be that it saved Scotland from catastrophe. The Irish famine was the greatest social disaster that overtook any Western European country in modern times. Out of a population of about eight and a half millions in 1845, something like half a million died of hunger and disease during the famine years and another million and a half emigrated. When the census was taken in 1851 it appeared that the total population had fallen by one-fifth and that of the rural areas by one quarter. Scotland had her share of sufferings, especially in the Highlands and Islands, at the same period, but in comparison her lot was happy. A recent writer has pointed out that during the latter part of the eighteenth century many people in the Highland area had acquired alongside their subsistence farming a slowly expanding money income through the sale of cattle, kelp, linen yarn and fish in southern markets. After 1815 this expansion of money incomes stopped abruptly and a price fall set in with painful consequences for many. The redundancy of population which was shown up so disastrously when the potato crops failed in the 1840's was almost as much a matter of diminution of money income as of increase of population.[96] Even so, if Scotland had remained a predominantly agricultural land, as she was sixty or seventy years earlier, it is hard to see how she could have avoided the fate of Ireland, confronted with the stark alternatives of emigration or starvation. If Scotland did in large measure escape that fate it was not through any foresight on the part of her rulers or the mass of the people, but through the resource of men like James Watt and David Dale who had devised new and improved instruments of production and new methods of organizing industry. Such men were partly impelled by motives relating to their own advancement in wealth and social station; but as we have seen in the case of Dale the motive of relieving the economic distress of their fellows was consciously present also, and, one may add, the motive of mastering difficulties and getting things done that had never been done before.

On the whole, men like Dale seem to have been empirical in

their economic views: nor would it be fair to say that they had formulated their general preference for economic freedom into a systematic philosophy of *laissez-faire*. No doubt the climate of opinion was favourable to such a philosophy. As early as 1730 the poet Pope had set forth a doctrine which must have been congenial to the *entrepreneur*:

> 'That Reason, Passion, answer one great aim;
> That true SELF-LOVE and SOCIAL are the same.'[97]

It must be added, however, that the current of affairs in the later eighteenth century in Scotland seemed to confirm that doctrine. The problem of the age was how to provide for a growing population, and in consequence, as we have seen, to interested observers like the parish ministers the man who established a factory was a patriot and the man who, at the same time, paid some heed to the education, health, and morals of his workers was a benevolent philanthropist. Men like Dale, the greatest *entrepreneurs* of the early phase of the Industrial Revolution in Scotland, carried on a tradition of philanthropy or paternal care, if one prefers to put it so, that was older and more deeply rooted than any Owenite humanitarianism. One may agree with a recent writer that 'there seems at the moment to be less danger of exaggerating the sense of responsibility that the best *entrepreneurs* possessed than of assuming that their outlook was typified by the worst'.[98]

2

PROGRESS AND POVERTY

SOCIAL concern always came naturally to Scottish churchmen; but there were developments early in our period which were calculated to stimulate it to an unusual degree. It would not be accurate to designate these developments simply as the agrarian and industrial revolutions. Some of the social changes involved in these revolutions were certainly such as to cause concern; but in general the changes aroused gratitude and hope. There came a time, however, when a situation of paradox, both perplexing and disquieting, made its appearance on the Scottish social scene. Until the 1820's the improvement in the general condition of the people of Scotland seemed to argue that the agrarian and industrial revolutions were a decidedly satisfactory development; but about that time the condition of a considerable proportion of the population showed decided deterioration, and there stood revealed a state of squalor and degradation that was without precedent. The elucidation of this paradox will explain the rise of much social concern.

The first official census was not taken till 1801, but tolerably reliable estimates of the population of Scotland exist for three periods in the eighteenth century, and there can be no doubt that there was not only a steady increase in the population but that there was also a rising rate of increase, despite considerable emigration, especially in the second half of the century.[1] Several factors have been adduced to account for this increase. The medical factors—improvements in midwifery, the founding of hospitals and dispensaries, the influence of popular books on medicine, the decline of certain diseases such as ague or malaria, the control of smallpox by inoculation—must have had beneficial results making for a lowering of the general death-rate. Modern study, however, suggests that of these medical factors the two last named were themselves dependent on the increasing prosperity of the countryside which resulted from the agricultural

improvements.[2] There is also much evidence that in the first
half of the eighteenth century, even apart from years of dearth,
the diet of the common people was seriously deficient, and that
they usually showed the unhealthy appearance and lethargic
attitude which modern observers attribute to malnutrition.
The great improvement in these respects in the later years of the
century is a frequent subject of comment in the Old Statistical
Account. Behind this improvement in the health of the people
lay a fuller and more varied diet, and behind that salutary change
lay the early agricultural improvements such as the abolition of
the infield and outfield system, the rotation of crops, the growing
of winter feed for cattle, enclosures and long leases. In the light
of a detailed discussion of these factors a recent writer already
quoted reaches this conclusion: 'In the study of so large a movement as this increase in population throughout the eighteenth
century we must look for an equally large force as the cause.
The only factor which has been shown which meets this re-
quirement is the improvement in the nutrition of the people.
Increase in medical knowledge and the waning of certain diseases
may have had some effect, but it can only have been subsidiary.'[3]
So much, then, for one side of the paradox—the improvement
in the general condition of the people of Scotland during the
eighteenth century and especially in its closing decades and the
early decades of the following century.

On the other hand from about 1820 onwards there emerged
an increasing undertone of indignant or doleful comment which
came to a climax in the controversies of the 1840's. Some of the
factors which account for this turning of a critical eye upon social
developments are obvious. As we of the twentieth century know
full well, a post-war period with its cessation of wartime spending
was sure to give rise to much dislocation and distress. The political agitations arising from this distress, typified by Peterloo in
England and the Radical War in Scotland, provoked question-
ings about the condition of the masses. Epidemics, not simply of
smallpox, which chiefly affected young persons, but also of
typhus, which attacked the wage-earners and so upset the industrial machine, and even of cholera, which might deal its
blows anywhere, caused widespread alarm. The stimulus of fear
—fear of disease, fear of social revolution—turned the eyes
of the ruling and professional classes toward the squalor and

destitution of the 'lower orders', and what they discovered was soon made public in printed pamphlets and reports.

The towns of Scotland had long been more unhealthy places than the rural areas, but, since the urban death-rate which had been falling for two or three generations showed a tendency to increase after 1820, we must conclude that they were becoming more unhealthy than for some time past.[4] Part of the reason was the density of the buildings in which the inhabitants lived. In 1818 a medical man in Glasgow remarked: 'An important step towards ventilation would be effected if we could even open up the lanes in which the lower classes live. In Glasgow the hovels which they inhabit are collected into dense masses of very great size between some of the larger streets. I believe it would greatly add to the healthiness of the place if some improvement which I have heard talked of were effected and straight and wide streets carried in different directions through these depositaries [sic] of wretchedness.'[5] How this density of dwellings arose is not hard to imagine. As the people seeking employment crowded into the towns, the well-to-do deserted the older parts and built themselves new dwellings in the outskirts. The old houses with their rooms divided and sometimes subdivided became the refuge of the newcomers; and, ere long, as the influx continued, the courts and gardens which had provided air and light in former times were built over, and even cellars were brought into use as dwelling places. Thus, though there was some expansion of the towns and cities and increase of their housing accommodation towards the end of the eighteenth and the beginning of the nineteenth century, the increase failed to keep pace with the much more rapid growth of population.

Not only were the buildings too close together but they also became grossly overcrowded. Another medical man, referring to those who suffered in a recent epidemic, wrote about 'the overcrowded state of their houses, families of six, eight and ten individuals crowded into one small apartment, without a bed to lie upon, if we except perhaps a quantity of long used straw or filthy rags . . . those small apartments being often let by the week are filthy in the extreme.'[6] It was sometimes observed too that the increase of urban population was due to immigration from the rural areas, and that the newcomers were generally not to be compared in quality with the older population. George

Lewis, writing in 1841 about the changed character of Dundee, remarked that 'the original Scottish population of Dundee, wherever they are found, even in the worst neighbourhoods, exhibit the best characteristics of the days of Willison. . . . It is not the native population but the imports of Dundee during the last twenty years that have changed its character. Its rising trade and manufacturing enterprise attracted for many years all comers, with a character or without one, like the army that followed David in his youthful exile—"Everyone that was in distress". . . . They came empty and destitute of good, and have too often remained so. When they came and settled the Church and the country were asleep and unprepared to bless them . . . the extensive parish of St. David's, with its 9,264 souls, has still only one Christian church of all denominations.'[7] In a paper read before the British Association in 1840 it was stated: 'It is quite obvious from these tables that the increase of population in Glasgow has arisen in a very great degree from immigration, and that from the increased demand for female domestic servants and for female labour in the numerous cotton and power-loom factories and bleachfields in the neighbourhood of the city, a large proportion of the immigrants have been females. . . . In 1819 there was one Irish person out of every 9·67 of the inhabitants; and in 1831 one out of every 5·69.'[8]

This influx of population from Ireland introduced another factor in the situation. In 1851 one in fourteen of the population of Scotland was Irish-born; twelve per cent. of the population of the ten chief towns, and eighteen per cent. of the population of Glasgow were Irish-born; and if account be taken of the children of these immigrants born in Scotland the proportion of Irish must have been substantially higher in each case.[9] This alien population complicated most social problems, not least those of poverty and overcrowding.

One class of houses soon drew the attention of medical observers as being distributing centres of disease—the common lodging-houses; and in the nature of things they were also nests of poverty, vice, and crime. 'The lodging-houses', wrote Dr. Cowan, 'are the media through which the newly arrived immigrants find their way to the Fever Hospital; and it is remarkable how many of the inmates of that hospital coming from lodging-houses have not been six months in the city.'[10]

The unenviable pre-eminence of Glasgow in the social problems of the period is to be attributed to that rapid development of industry there which brought about a diminution in the relative proportion of the wealthier and middle class and made Charles Baird, the lawyer who wrote the survey of the condition of Glasgow for Edwin Chadwick's Sanitary Inquiry, state that 'at least four-fifths of the population of the city of Glasgow and suburbs consist of the working classes and their families.'[11] The same shrewd observer noted that lower in the social scale than what could properly be called the working classes came 'the poor who have no regular employment or sufficient means of subsistence'. The former, however, he also noted, were subject to many vicissitudes by which even the most prudent and economical might be reduced to penury, for example 'the sudden convulsions and fluctuations of trade, by which the means of subsistence are frequently withdrawn from large masses; the high price of provisions; and above all their liability to diseases, especially those of an epidemic nature'.[12]

Further light upon the way of life of those at the base of the social pyramid may be gained from the statements of the Reverend John Smith, one-time Congregational minister at Ayr and then joint-founder and editor of the *Glasgow Examiner*, who writing in 1846 said: 'On inquiry we find that in Glasgow from 5,000 to 10,000 persons are nightly accommodated in twopenny and threepenny lodging-houses. We have in our possession a list containing no fewer than 489 of such houses. . . . Though only 489 have been registered, not fewer than 600 or 700 exist; and as some of these houses have as many as 30 lodgers nightly, and others but 2, were we to assume the number of houses to be 600, and the average of their lodgers to be 10, we should have an aggregate and average of 6,000 nightly in these cheap houses.'[13] Another statement of the same zealous investigator deserves notice—'by a careful and extensive induction we have arrived at the appalling conclusion that at least 20,000 of the inhabitants live on charity and theft'.[14] He was also of opinion that the chief of the causes making for the dissemination of poverty and crime throughout Glasgow was 'the untenantable dwellings of the city'. In an appeal to the city authorities he maintained that they already had power to demolish such dwellings on the score of insufficiency or unhealthiness, and he reinforced his appeal by summarizing the conclusions of his investigations thus: 'It has been indisputably proved that the dwellings of the lower classes are altogether untenantable, and that they are nests of disease and crime. We have stated the size and appearance of the dwellings and the number and character of the inhabitants. We have proven that our paupers on the parish roll do not receive a sufficiency to pay their rents, and consequently they have absolutely nothing to furnish their daily supplies, unless what occasional charity or theft supplies them. We have proven that the labouring man pays double the rent that his small earnings warrant, and that, after all, he is sheltered in cabins unfit to lodge cattle. We have proved that several parts of the city abound with filthy lanes, which lead to houses inaccessible to the light or air of heaven, and that in these places wretched females are huddled together in tens and hundreds.'[15] A medical observer a little earlier wrote: 'The streets or rather lanes and alleys in which the poor live are filthy beyond measure: excrementitious matter and filth of every description is allowed to lay [sic] upon the lanes, or, if collected, it remains accumulating for months, until the landlord whose property it is, is pleased to remove it. The houses are ruinous, ill-constructed and to an incredible degree destitute of furniture. In many there is not an article of bedding and the body clothes of the inmates are of the most revolting description.'[16]

Two further pictures from the outspoken investigator previously quoted may help to stress the moral implications of these physical conditions. 'For an apartment 10 feet by 6 James Martin, a labourer, pays £3. 5s. rent. For similar apartments in this close rents varying from £3 to £4 are annually paid. In some of these 6 and sometimes 8 persons are nightly sheltered, the rents being so high as to compel the tenants to take in lodgers. The visiting missionary gives a melancholy account of the dwellers in this close. Instead of fining the inmates for keeping disorderly houses, it might be advisable to fine the landlords for knowingly year after year letting them to such.' Again, 'No. 93 High Street, better known by the name of Pipe-house close, a most densely-peopled locality, contains about 150 families, and taking five as the average in each, it will give 750. A friend of mine stood about an hour the other Sabbath morning, looking at a wee pawn in the close, and in that short period he saw no fewer than 50 persons pop in. In an entry near by he saw men, women and children stripping their coats, petticoats, jackets, frocks, shoes etc. Nearly opposite the pawn there is a spirit-cellar which, under the name of selling milk, catches, with scarcely an exception, all the wee pawn dupes and wrings from them the last farthing. Attached to this spirit-cellar there is a dunghill which yields a great revenue. It frequently overflows and then all around is one scene of filth and pollution.'[17]

Dirt and misery in Edinburgh, though more circumscribed in area, were not essentially different. Dr. George Bell, a medical man, reported that: 'In one room, twelve feet long by ten broad, we once saw twelve women asleep. There was not even straw for them to lie on; . . . They had no covering save the rags in which they wandered about during the day. We awoke one of the sleepers, an old Irishwoman, and asked her some questions. She paid a penny per night for the privilege of sleeping in this den. She lived by begging, and charity makes us suppose that all the rest did the same.'[18]

Evil conditions which were at their maximum in Glasgow and Edinburgh were not lacking in other smaller centres. In Dumfries it was reported that 'the residences of the poorer classes in the town consist generally of one apartment only, so that in many instances it is necessarily overcrowded and when any contagious sickness arises, facilitates much the propagation of disease. There are several poor lodging-houses to which vagrants resort, and where the beds and their occupants are crowded into a very small space. . . . It is quite common to find pigsties in close contiguity with the houses, and even instances have occurred of pigs being kept within the house.'[19] Of the houses of the poorest of the population of Ayr it is said: 'There is usually a bedstead at each side of the door, often much shattered, beneath which all sorts of rubbish and lumber are huddled together, and also the store of potatoes for the family when they possess so much wealth. Nay we sometimes detect a heap of horse-dung under the bed, which is collected by the children from the streets, and sold when a sufficient quantity has been accumulated. As to cleaning under the beds, this is never dreamt of, nor would it be easily effected, as they are generally closeted in upon three sides.'[20] In Stirling, the report described how 'the filth of the gaols, containing on an average sixty-five prisoners, is floated down the public streets every second or third day. . . . The lower part of a dwelling-house, not more than three or four yards from the town-house and gaol, is used as a "midding" and pig-sty, the filth being thrown into it by the window and door. . . . The closes where the poor dwell, and where accumulations of filth most abound are, I may safely say, utterly neglected by the scavengers.'[21] The report from Greenock was particularly vivid. 'There is one poor man who was under my care in the hospital with asthma for six months, he was dismissed as incurable and is now living with his wife and seven children in a dark room on the ground-floor more fit for a coal-cellar than a human being; it is lighted by a fixed window about two feet square; the breadth of the room is only four feet and the length eight. There is only one bed for the whole family, and yet the rent of this hole is £5.' Again, 'Behind my consulting rooms, where I am now sitting, there is a large dunghill with a privy attached; to my knowledge that dunghill has not been emptied for six months; it serves a whole neighbourhood, and the effluvium is so offensive that I cannot open the window.'[22]

In estimating the incidence of poverty and disease it must be remembered that the industries which attracted the newcomers to the towns were liable to slumps, strikes, and lockouts, when unemployment and consequent poverty brought acute suffering to thousands. Moreover, the destitution characteristic of these periods meant diminished resistance in the constitution of the sufferers and provided conditions favourable for epidemic dis-eases. Medical observers were not slow to note a connexion be-tween the epidemics and the destitution of the masses. 'The tables given of the number of fever patients in each year will prove that the years in which they are most numerous are those in which destitution most prevailed, and thus demonstrate that destitution and fever are inseparably linked together.'[23] Modern investigation has confirmed the soundness of this judgment by establishing a correlation between the epidemics and the indus-trial depressions. The historian of Britain's epidemics wrote with reference to Glasgow: 'The worst year of the series for fever was 1837 and the worst month of that year was May when the fever deaths were 1 in 3·22 of the mortality from all causes. That great access of fever in Glasgow followed immediately upon the great strike of the cotton-spinners on 8 April 1837 by which eight thousand persons, mostly women, were thrown out of work.'[24] Of relapsing fever in Scotland in 1842-4 it is reported that 'all accounts agree in stating that the epidemic supervened upon a period of great distress among the Scottish poor and that it was restricted throughout to the poorest and most wretched of the population'.[25] One further testimony to the same effect may be added: 'In 1817 to 1819 when fever first prevailed to an alarming extent, its ravages were preceded by two bad harvests and want of employment for the labouring poor.'[26]

Here, then, is the other side of the paradoxical situation—while the general condition of the people of Scotland had improved in the eighteenth century and continued to improve in the nineteenth, there were large sections of the increasing town and city population whose condition deteriorated for a period in the first half of the nineteenth century. The developments which led to the vast expansion of the urban population had begun in the eighteenth century, but it took some time for the full effects to become obvious; and when they did, social concern, prompted both by benevolence and by fear, became apparent in the ruling classes. Dr. Cowan was quite frank about the matter when he wrote: 'In 1826 to 1828, 1831-2, 1837-8, when large sums were voluntarily raised, and in 1832 under the cholera assessment acts for the relief of the unemployed and sick poor, it was the previous existence of fever and the dread of cholera that instigated the benevolent deed.'[27]

What remains a problem is why, when the seriousness of the situation began to be realized, the steps taken to deal with it were so slow and half-hearted. To take a single example, the first Medical Officers of Health were not appointed for Edinburgh and Glasgow till 1862 and 1863 respectively. There was, indeed, a large amount of help organized in the most acute emergencies —soup kitchens, relief committees, charitable funds, improvised fever hospitals and the like—but generally these measures fell into abeyance when the emergency was over, and the same process had to be gone through the next time to call them into activity again. Some of the factors involved may be enumerated. First, it may be taken for granted that, despite the publicity given by the writings of the reformers, there were many citizens who did not know what was going on in the lower quarters of their towns. This should cause no surprise to those who, in face of all the social interest and agitation of past generations, were

taken aback when the temporary evacuation at the outbreak of
the Second World War revealed the way of life of a substantial
section of the population. Second, it may be taken as certain
that many hard-hearted persons, who had reason to know what
was happening, refused to concern themselves about it, or stilled
their consciences with a donation to a relief fund. Charles Baird,
the Glasgow lawyer, was quite blunt about this. 'The higher
classes', he wrote, 'are at present far too indifferent to the condition of the poor. They pronounce them reckless, discontented,
dissolute, and degraded; but were their wretched abodes and
their general condition minutely examined, the surprise would
be that they were not more reckless and discontented: and were
their abodes and the general condition of the poor improved, we
would not only have less misery and wretchedness, but also less
tumult and crime in our land.'[28]

Third, it was more difficult for the ruling classes in Scotland
to appreciate the seriousness of the new situation and to stir
themselves to take effectual remedial action, for Scotland, as
compared with England, had been plunged more suddenly into
industrial development and from a more primitive economic and
social state, where dearth, disease, and miserable housing had
been all too usual. Fourth, while the English poor-law system,
both before and after its reform in 1834, had serious faults, it
was effective in preventing acute destitution: hence the reformers in England could concentrate, as Chadwick did, on
sanitary measures. In Scotland, as we have seen, the reformers,
who were often medical men, were perfectly aware of the sanitary and public health deficiencies; but they were diverted to the
subject of destitution by the inadequacies of the Scottish system
of dealing with the poor and by the Alison-Chalmers controversy about it. Vigorous attention to sanitation and the control
of epidemics was delayed till twenty years after the new Poor
Law Act of 1845. For this delay, too, one is driven to seek an
explanation, and that leads to a fifth factor, the lack of administrative machinery capable of dealing with the manifold aspects
of the urban situation. Municipal government in the cities was a
patchwork of unco-ordinated and even competing authorities.
The reformers soon saw the ineffectiveness of such a system, but
it took a long time to get it remedied. In 1840 Dr. Cowan was
lamenting in Glasgow that 'over the city and suburbs there are

four independent magistracies and boards of police, four assessments for the poor's-rates, and four modes of administering the poor's funds, equally independent of one another. . . . To remedy the evils one municipal government, one police board, one mode of assessment and one uniform mode of distributing the poor's funds are imperiously demanded to check crime and diminish disease and pauperism. Centralization would increase the efficiency of all the above boards. But besides the criminal police of the district, a sanitary police is also requisite, and for this purpose much more extensive powers should be vested in the police than they at present possess.'[29] The origin of these irrational procedures in local government lay in that expansion of the towns which brought into existence new suburbs outside the area subject to the old town councils which, until the Burgh Reform Act of 1833, were corrupt self-perpetuating oligarchies. These new areas required services such as watching, lighting, cleansing, and paving and to meet such needs new organs of local government were improvised piecemeal outside the old system. It nevertheless persisted, and when it had received something of the vitality of a representative system by burgh reform it began gradually to gather into its hands the control of all aspects of local government throughout the whole area of the town or city. That process, however, was protracted, possibly because the suburban dwellers, content with having made provision for their own needs, were in no hurry to bring themselves under the town council and have to contribute towards similar provision for the whole city.

Sixth, between the first Reform Act of 1832 and the appointment of a Secretary for Scotland in 1885 the Home Secretary, advised by the Lord Advocate, held the ministerial responsibility for Scottish affairs. Scotland lacked not only a legislature, but even a centre of administration. That in itself tended to delays, to irresponsibility on the part of Scottish local authorities, and to a reluctance to accept new organs of centralized control when the centre was London. Recent writers have pointed out, for instance, that the Public Health (Scotland) Bill, 1848, which would have put local boards of health in Scotland under the superintendence of the Secretary of the General Board of Health already in existence in London, was dropped in face of Scottish opposition based partly on criticism by Scottish medical men of the theories about epidemic disease which guided the London Board, and partly on the reasonable feeling that a better plan would be to have a General Board for Scotland consisting of persons conversant with the law and customs of Scotland.[30]

Seventh, another factor in the situation may have been the current economic doctrine of *laissez-faire*. The influence of this, one may, however, suspect, has been exaggerated. Influential men in the early part of the century were by no means reluctant, when it suited them, to appeal to Parliament for compulsory powers, as is witnessed by the long series of Police Acts obtained by the Scottish burghs, beginning even before the nineteenth century. The fault of these Acts seems to have been not so much the meagre nature of the powers they conveyed, but the lack both of vigorous administration through a sufficiently numerous, trained, and responsible staff, and of constant direction and supervision by some central body authorized by the central government. On the other hand when some vested interest of the well-to-do was in question, the parties concerned found in current economic theory a potent argument in favour of the rights of property.

The relation between theory and practice in these matters is difficult to define. Sometimes it seems as if the currently accepted theory were a rationalization of the practice which was already being modified. At all events there is an element of paradox in the movement of economic theory within our period. In the early part of it the current popular explanation of economic happenings was in terms of the cosmic pattern set forth in the Newtonian astronomy. Men thought of the heavenly bodies maintaining their calm and orderly course under the control of the one basic principle of gravitation, and by analogy they thought of individual men meeting in a common market and quietly but inevitably adjusting the prices of labour and commodities under the control of one basic principle—that of self-interest. Later, the popular explanation under Marxian and Darwinian influences took on a more 'tooth and claw', survival of the fittest pattern. The element of paradox emerges in the fact that in the earlier period, when economic hardness was indeed being endured and many were literally failing to survive, the current explanation of economic happenings was less in terms of conflict than in the later period—from the mid-century onwards into the seventies

—when in fact conditions were easier and, since the State was intervening more for the restraint of the strong and the protection of the weak and the positive welfare of the community, an explanation in terms of a new picture seemed to be required.

3

PIONEERS IN COUNTRY AND CITY

THE Industrial Revolution with the rapid increase of population in towns and cities and all the concomitant problems overtook Scotland with startling suddenness. Observers like the parish ministers who wrote the parish surveys for the Old Statistical Account were well aware of what was happening, and they were not unaware of the problems arising, but in view of the primitive economic and social state out of which Scotland was emerging their doubts and hesitations were overshadowed by their welcome of the new situation and its possibilities. It is not surprising, therefore, that they had no novel or general remedies to suggest for the ills that they could not fail to notice. What they did seek to promote were piecemeal measures evoked by local problems, though some of these measures proved to have a more than local application. One example from the country and one from the city will show how earnest men were provoked to good works in their own situation.

Henry Duncan, born in 1774, a son of the manse, was educated at Dumfries Academy and the University of St. Andrews and was employed for three years with a mercantile firm in Liverpool. Turning to the ministry he studied divinity at Edinburgh and Glasgow and was ordained and inducted to the parish of Ruthwell in 1799.[1] He became Moderator of the General Assembly forty years later and, as one of the leaders of the Evangelical party, he was associated with Thomas Chalmers in the Disruption and in the formation of the Free Church of Scotland. Forsaking his church, manse, and grounds, he became minister of the Free Church at Ruthwell and died there in 1846.

His son records that an incident which took place in the summer of 1804 may be regarded as 'in some measure the turning-point of his religious character'. This was a meeting with three Quaker 'approved preachers', one of whom, Mrs. Deborah Darby, was also a formative influence in the life of Elizabeth Fry.

4

It is significant that the outcome in both cases was the same—an ardent philanthropy.[2] Duncan was a versatile man of more than common ability. At the time of a threatened French invasion he raised and captained a company of volunteers from his parish. He discovered and restored the runic cross of Ruthwell and made some significant contributions to geology. Besides founding and editing a local newspaper, he published several tales and he has the credit, along with William Oliphant, of having founded in 1808 the *Scottish Cheap Repository*—the pioneer of popular monthly magazines—of which he was the first editor.[3]

In his rural parish Duncan soon found opportunities of proving himself a friend of the poor. At the end of the eighteenth century a series of bad harvests had raised the price of food to famine levels. Through his brothers in Liverpool he ordered a cargo of Indian corn, which was landed at a little creek near Ruthwell and sold at cost price in quantities varying with the size of the family.[4] He also brought flax from Dumfries in his own phaeton for the women of the parish to spin in their own houses. His name, however, is chiefly associated with the initiation of Savings Banks.

Such institutions seem to have originated in Germany in the latter part of the eighteenth century. In England a beginning was made about the turn of the century by the Rev. Joseph Smith at Wendover and Mrs. Priscilla Wakefield at Tottenham. Henry Duncan, writing of himself as founder of the parish bank at Ruthwell, told how, about the beginning of the year 1810, he 'had been anxiously employed in examining different plans which had from time to time been suggested for ameliorating the condition of the lower orders, and in the course of his inquiries, he happened to meet with a pamphlet giving an account of a scheme, called by the inventor "Tranquillity", of a nature perhaps too complicated for general adoption. One of the proposed provisions of this plan, however, was an Economical Bank for the reception of the small savings of the industrious. The benefit which might result from carrying a plan of this latter kind into effect immediately appeared to him in a very strong light and he determined, as the best means of ultimately introducing it to general notice, to try in the first place the effect of its operation in the very contracted sphere of his own parish.'[5]

Ruthwell, being a poor rural parish with no more than 1,100 in its population, may have seemed an unfavourable sphere for an experiment of this kind, but Duncan was impressed with both the material and the moral benefit which might accrue to his people, and on 10 May 1810 the little parish savings bank commenced operations. The initial success was such that ere many months had passed other places had begun to follow the Ruthwell lead. To overcome the suspicions of the people a box was used fitted with three different locks which could be opened only in the presence of the three persons possessed of the appropriate keys. The first year the deposits amounted to £151, the second to £176, the third to £241, and then progress became more rapid, for by the fourth year deposits came to £922, and by 16 December 1814 to £1,164. 9s. 3d.[6] To make the venture widely known Duncan in 1815 issued a pamphlet entitled *An Essay on the Nature and Advantages of Parish Banks*. By 1818 there were, outside Edinburgh and Glasgow, 130 popular savings banks in Scotland with about a thousand members and £30,000 in deposits.[7] Then Duncan resolved to strengthen and encourage such banks by getting government protection for them. The legislature first turned its attention to the matter in 1817 when the first Savings Bank Acts were passed; but these applied to England and Ireland. Duncan, accordingly, drafted a bill suitable for Scotland, and spent time and money in London in propaganda for it, with the result that an Act for the Protection of Banks for Savings in Scotland became law in July 1819. It was largely through his advocacy also that another Act was passed in 1835 which, among other provisions, gave greater security to Scottish Savings Banks by extending to them the privilege, which those in England had previously received, of investing their funds with the National Debt Commissioners. The result was an immediate increase in the number of such banks in Scotland.

The initiation of Savings Banks may appear today a very small and unimportant social reform. Two things, however, may tend to modify that judgment. First, the ordinary banks in those days did not accept deposits of less than £10, and thus the only bank for poor and thrifty folk was a stocking-foot, a chink in the wall, or a space beneath a loose floor-board, with all the temptations and dangers involved. Second, Duncan, like his friend and younger contemporary, Thomas Chalmers, was opposed to legal assessments for poor relief,[8] and in favour of the traditional

Scottish voluntary system. Thus while his founding of the parish
bank at Ruthwell was in the first place a measure designed to
meet the immediate need of his parishioners, the wider possibilities were in his mind from the first. His enthusiastic promotion of Savings Banks was but part of that whole policy of
quickening and extending the agencies of the Church in manageable parishes which was the answer of Chalmers and the Evangelical party in the Church of Scotland to the questions of their
day. In that connexion it is significant that Thomas Guthrie, an
Evangelical leader of the succeeding generation, who in tackling
his parish of St. John's in Edinburgh sought to follow the lead of
Chalmers,[9] shortly after going to the parish of Arbirlot in 1830
established a savings bank and conducted it himself, while
several of the principal farmers in the parish acted as trustees
along with him. 'I was the entire manager,' he wrote, 'giving out
money only on Saturday evening, the regular time for its transactions, and that only on a fortnight's notice—but receiving it
in the shape of a shilling, the lowest deposit, at any time and
any day, Sunday, of course, excepted.'[10] However inadequate
their solution, these men were confronting the problem of the
condition of the people or, to use Duncan's words characteristic
of the age, of 'ameliorating the condition of the lower orders'.
The problem, however, as it met Duncan in Ruthwell was slight
in bulk compared with its colossal proportions as it confronted
his older contemporary in Glasgow.

Stevenson Macgill was born in 1765 at Port Glasgow where his
father was a shipbuilder. It was perhaps important for his later
evangelical outlook that there were Methodist influences in his
family. His father was a native of Dunbar and had been appren-
ticed to a shipbuilder. One week-day evening when he was
about the age of seventeen he happened to go along with a com-
rade to a Methodist prayer-meeting held by a group of pious
soldiers who had just returned from Germany and were encamped
at Dunbar. A definite religious impression was made on him,
and along with his companion he joined the Methodists and kept
up his connexion with them till his death in 1804.

Stevenson Macgill was presented to the parish of Eastwood in
1791 and translated to the Tron parish of Glasgow in 1797. In
1814 he was appointed Professor of Divinity at Glasgow, and
was succeeded in the Tron by Thomas Chalmers. Unlike

Chalmers, Macgill was not a great preacher nor an outstanding leader; but he was equally a man of large-hearted benevolence and practical insight into the needs of the unfortunate. Indeed it may well be maintained that he had, though an older man than Chalmers, a more practical and up-to-date insight into the rapidly changing social situation in the early decades of the nineteenth century. His biographer says: 'Dr. Macgill was not one of those puling sentimentalists who imagine that a protestant minister has nothing to do with the great public events of the times, or the influence of civil government on the habits and conditions of men.'[11] He was convinced, says the same authority, 'that much of the usefulness and efficacy of a minister's labours in a city depend on the attention which is paid to the physical wants of the people, and on the vigilance of a well-regulated police in watching over the health and morals of the whole community. These considerations led him early to attach himself to the public institutions of the city, and he soon became generally known and respected as their guardian and their guide.'[12]

When Macgill came as a minister to Glasgow in 1797 the population was between seventy and eighty thousand: by the time he left his parish for a professor's chair in 1814 it had grown to well over one hundred thousand: and by the time of his death in 1840 it was still increasing, by about ten thousand a year, and was approaching the three hundred thousand mark. In those circumstances he quickly came to the same conclusion as Chalmers did a little later, that the rapidly expanding population required the provision of more parish churches and more parish schools. By 1809, if not earlier, he was contending for this in the Presbytery of Glasgow, and that church court did indeed at that time strongly recommend the erection of three additional churches for the city.[13] Unfortunately, as a writer put it a generation later, 'the city dignitaries of the day were more intent upon the great wars of the continent and the movements in the peninsula than those evils around them that required no far-seeing sagacity to detect.'[14]

Labouring in vain as regards religious and educational provision, Macgill had considerable success in carrying into effect some of his views regarding the physical and moral equipment of a large and growing city. He seems to have been the pioneer of prison-reform in Scotland. His pamphlet, *Remarks on Prisons*, published in 1809, abounds in enlightened suggestions about the classification of prisoners, their employment and instruction, the planning of buildings so that different classes of prisoners may be kept separate, the removal of all possibility of jailers' making gain by selling things, especially strong drink, to the prisoners. His admirable suggestions, it appears, were not acted upon in the new prison built in Glasgow about this time, but they were used in the construction of the county prison at Paisley.[15] Macgill took more than a theoretical interest in such matters, for we hear of his having established a library in the Glasgow prison for the use of the inmates.[16]

Macgill was also a pioneer in the care of the insane in the West of Scotland. Until the beginning of the nineteenth century there was no proper provision in Glasgow for the treatment of the insane. There were, indeed, some wards in the Town's Hospital set apart for such sufferers, but they were insufficient in number and size for the humane guardianship let alone for the cure of the patients. They were in fact cold and damp cells, mere places of restraint. Early in the century the directors of the Town's Hospital appointed a Committee to consider the state of the lunatic wards, and soon plans were drawn for a separate building calculated to accommodate about one hundred and twenty persons and to serve the whole West of Scotland. Provision was planned for two classes of inmates, those who could pay their board and those who were paupers; and the patients were to be distributed according to four classifications—frantic, incurable, ordinary patients, and convalescents. In 1804 a beginning was made with collecting funds, and by the time the foundation stone was laid in August 1810 more than £7,000 had been gathered in Glasgow alone.[17] On that occasion Macgill preached a sermon in which he showed a remarkably enlightened understanding of the problems involved.[18] The asylum, situated in Parliamentary Road, was opened in December 1814 when twenty-three men and eighteen women were transferred to it from the cells of the Town's Hospital. Its object was declared to be 'to promote, at the same time, the security, cure and comfort of the insane', and for a generation it served its purpose until it gave place to the more extensive institution at Gartnavel, of which the foundation stone was laid in 1842.

While the first suggestion of such an institution in Glasgow seems to have been made by Robert McNair of Belvedere, Macgill was described as 'one of the directors and eminent promoters', and we may assume that his published views were reflected in its constitution, rules and practice. At the time it was regarded as the best of its kind in Britain, and a modern writer has commented thus: 'A reading of the earlier reports of the hospital suggests that this was from the beginning conducted on humane and enlightened lines. Harshness and coercion on the part of the attendants were condemned, as were also depleting methods of treatment such as blood-letting. An ample diet, fresh air, exercise, occupation and amusements, and sedatives to calm the mind were repeatedly mentioned as remedial measures. It was recognized that one of the most beneficial factors in the treatment of the insane was daily occupation, and there were occupational workshops. . . . There were billiard rooms and a library; and Dr. Hutcheson stressed the importance of reading and music as therapeutic measures.'[19]

Another subject on which Macgill held views in advance of his time was the restoration of delinquents. While he was still a parish minister he formed a Glasgow Society for the Encouragement of Penitents with two objects, 'first, to preserve boys who have fallen into crimes from returning to their idle and pernicious courses: second, to protect and encourage penitent females in their desire for reformation.'[20] The second of these was first dealt with through the founding of the Magdalene Asylum which, says his biographer, 'owed its existence entirely to the persevering exertions' of Macgill. He preached at the opening of it in 1815, and by 1819 he was in a position not only to report a gratifying measure of success but also to give a sketch of other desirable institutions of a similar nature. He proposed a House and School of Industry for women and a Work House in two divisions, one for delinquent boys and the other for men in lack of employment who through want and hopelessness might be driven to criminal courses.[21] At the time a beginning was made with these schemes, but it was not till after Macgill's death that they became firmly established.

The Scottish minister's traditional concern for education and the care of the poor was also prominent in his interests. He held progressive views about the poor, and wished provision to be made for the destitute and helpless, children as well as adults. His proposal was that 'small villages of well-aired cottages, in the neighbourhood of our cities, for poor and unfortunate persons, might sometimes be built for this purpose, and placed under the general superintendence of pious and humane individuals'.[22] In the case of poor people able in some degree to work for their subsistence or with friends willing to assist them 'the relief afforded by pensions is least expensive and most conducive to their happiness'. Unlike Chalmers, however, Macgill was not opposed to poor relief by the method of assessments.[23]

In 1819 Macgill seized an opportunity to carry his zeal for social welfare into a sphere wider than his own city. In the letter of the Prince Regent to the General Assembly of that year something was said about the alarming increase of crimes, and the fathers and brethren were exhorted to pay attention to the instruction of prisoners and the education of the young. In the Assembly's reply an assurance was given that the Church would attend to these matters. Striking while the iron was hot, Macgill rose and addressed the Assembly and secured unanimous agreement 'that a Committee be appointed to take under their consideration the most effectual measures for providing the means of religious instruction for unhappy persons confined in our prisons and bridewells and for the performance of religious worship in these places, and also for the education of the poor, particularly in large and populous cities'.[24] The Committee, with Macgill as Convener, held several meetings during the sittings of the Assembly, and such was his knowledge of the matters remitted to it that an interim report was presented to the Assembly before it closed. The Committee urged the Assembly to endeavour to secure for Scotland an Act of Parliament similar to one already passed for England and Wales providing for the appointment of prison chaplains and teachers, and to recommend ministers in parishes with prisons in them to be active in measures for the reform of prisoners. On the subject of education it urged the Assembly to promote the establishment of schools for elementary education in populous towns and cities, in addition to schools of higher education.[25] The report was approved and a Committee appointed with Macgill as Convener to proceed further in these matters. The outcome must have been disappointing to the Convener. More than once he was thanked by the Moderator in the name of the Assembly for his diligence, and his proposals won the approval of the Home Secretary and of the Lord Advocate, but apparently there was no enthusiasm for them among those who had it in their power to take effective action; and so though the Assembly's Committee on Prison Discipline and Burgh Schools, as it was called in 1823, continued to exist under the Convenership first of Macgill and then of Dr. Inglis nothing effective was done till much later.[26]

It was in 1819 also that Macgill gathered together some of his earlier writings and republished them along with others in the volume entitled *Discourses and Essays on Subjects of Public Interest*. Of this work H. M. B. Reid says: 'It suggests a re-valuation of Macgill's abilities from the economic point of view. Chalmers has carried off the honours, but Macgill perhaps deserved them.'[27] Perhaps he ought to get credit, too, for inspiring others with a social concern that issued in practical measures. It is surely significant that John Dunlop, the founder of the Temperance Movement, 'lived altogether eight years under Dr. Macgill's charge',[28] and that William Collins, publisher, temperance reformer and church extension pioneer, spent his youth at Eastwood and was wont to recall how Macgill, when minister there, used to come into the village school to encourage the teacher and address the children. It was with Macgill's encouragement that Collins came to Glasgow in 1813 and set up first as a teacher of a private school, becoming a member and then an elder of the Tron congregation under Macgill's ministry.[29] Again, the biographer of James Begg suggests that Begg consciously or unconsciously formed his social views on the model of those of Macgill who was his Professor of Theology at Glasgow. 'The very measures which Dr. Macgill continually advocated in the social department, relating to pauperism, the treatment of prisoners, education, and the economical elevation of the people, were the measures whose advocacy afterwards occupied much of the time and thought of Dr. Begg.'[30]

Macgill thus came into contact with three notable figures, Dunlop, Collins, and Begg, and one may surmise that they caught from him something of the social enthusiasm which he concealed beneath a stiffly dignified exterior, for the impression one forms of him is of a man of wide outlook, of shrewd judgement, and of humane and Christian principles, who was willing to bear the ridicule of the unconcerned and the obstruction of the lethargic and to move forward on a narrow front, if he could not move forward on a wide one, towards goals which his far-seeing wisdom had discerned.

4

THE SOCIAL POLICY
OF THOMAS CHALMERS

THE typical approach of Scottish churchmen to the changes involved in the agrarian and industrial revolutions may be discerned in Stevenson Macgill and Henry Duncan; but its merits and defects may be more clearly seen in Thomas Chalmers who became minister of the Tron parish of Glasgow in 1815, the year of Waterloo.

Chalmers was a great man who in his time played many parts —preacher and pastor, professor and ecclesiastical statesman, orator and philanthropist, theologian and economist. For him Glasgow opened a new range of experience, for hitherto he had been familiar with much smaller and quieter places—Anstruther his birthplace, St. Andrews his University town, and the rural parish of Kilmany in Fife. Intellectually he was conversant with the thought of his day in mathematics and science, in politics and economics; and about 1811 he had undergone an evangelical conversion which changed his former ambitions and gave him a new zeal for the Christian good of Scotland. His new sphere must have given a shock to a man whose experience was rural, whose instincts were conservative and whose religious outlook was evangelical. In that post-war Glasgow he found not only religious moderatism but sheer irreligion, not only liberalism but radicalism, not only a dense city population but destitution and demoralization.

Yet Chalmers was a success in Glasgow. His preaching drew crowds. The middle classes were captivated by his special courses of Thursday sermons designed to deal with the special needs of the time and the place—his Astronomical Discourses and his Commercial Discourses—both when they were delivered and when they were published. If Chalmers had been a lesser man and a less Christian man he might well have been content with the superficial success of a popular preacher and writer. In fact he was far from content. His zeal for the Christian good of his native land, his pastoral care for the people of his parish, and, be it added, his fear of the social unrest generated in the lowest ranks of society, moved him to face the problems of an industrialized Scotland. It was perhaps a pity that he did not face them simply in the light of his own observation and Christian compassion.

Chalmers was a true disciple of Adam Smith, in that he held that economic matters should be left open to the free and unshackled operation of natural forces. He wrote approvingly of Adam Smith's assertion that it were better for trade, and for the interest of the country, that every positive interference on the part of Government were done away; and for himself he declared: 'We would, in short, raise no positive apparatus whatever for the direct object of meeting and alleviating the ills of poverty. This we leave to the theorists; and we satisfy ourselves with simply asserting, that unfettered Nature, working in individuals, can do the thing better than regulation can. . . .'[1] Chalmers may with even greater propriety, however, be called a disciple of Malthus, who maintained that population when unchecked increased in geometrical ratio while food supplies increased merely in arithmetical ratio. The conclusion seemed inevitable that the alternative before humanity was either to limit the birth-rate by moral restraint or to let the population be kept within the bounds of available food by natural checks such as starvation and disease. The Malthusian view that there is a natural tendency for population to increase till it presses too heavily on the supply of food dominated the political economy of Chalmers and conditioned his attitude to proposals for betterment. Without the exercise of self-control by the masses, he held, no efforts to improve their condition could have more than a temporary success; and the only force able to produce in them the strength of character necessary for the practice of such self-control was Christian principle. Hence education, and primarily religious education, was the chief cure for the social ills of the age; and that meant bringing the people into closest contact with church and school.

Evidence of the pervasive influence of Malthusian conceptions in the outlook of Chalmers is not far to seek. He considered a State-aided scheme of emigration desirable, if used as a temporary auxiliary to the gradual abolition of the poor-law, but he argued against it by itself and as a permanent institution on the ground that it 'would stimulate population even beyond the relief which it could effectuate'.[2] Again, a significant clue to the basic assumptions of this implacable foe of State charity is found in the fact that, while willing to admit and even encourage State provision for disease,[3] he refused to extend it to include provision for old age.[4] No harm, he appeared to think, could result from people's knowledge that if they had a child which was blind or insane they might get legal charity for it or have it cared for in an institution supported by public money. That knowledge was not likely to increase early marriages or send up the birth-rate. Let them know, however, that if they become helpless through old age they will be supported by the State, and it would strike at the natural pieties and diminish the prudence and restraint of the poor. A charity which might increase the population and thus increase its beneficiaries is to be condemned. Thus the exception in favour of 'those varieties, whether of mental or of bodily disease, for which it is a wise and salutary thing to rear a public institution' is the exception which proved the rule.[5]

While Chalmers accepted the existing class structure of society as inevitable and right he was in no way opposed to a higher standard of living for the masses. 'It is our belief,' he wrote, 'that through the medium not of a political change in the State, but of a moral and personal change upon themselves, there is not one desirable amelioration which they might not mount their way to. . . . The condition to which they might hopefully aspire—and it is the part of every honest and enlightened philanthropist to help them forward to it—is that of less work and higher wages; and this, not only that they might participate more largely in the physical enjoyments of life, but that, in exemption from oppressive toil, and with the command of dignified leisure, there might be full opportunity and scope for the development of their nobler faculties in the prosecution of all the higher objects of a rational and immortal existence.'[6] Such a desirable state, however, could not come about simply by increasing wages. With higher wages there must be self-restraint on the part of the people as a whole: later marriage, leading to a diminished supply of labour and a rise in wages; and the practice of thrift and saving, leading to greater bargaining power. Such improvements, however, could never be simply given to the masses: they must be won through the exercise of their own frugal, industrious, and self-restrained habits, issuing from an adequate moral and religious training.

That, however, was a long-term policy. What of the immediate needs of the poor? Holding the economic views he did Chalmers was vehemently opposed to any legal right of maintenance. Voluntary kindness, not compulsory relief, seemed to him to be the remedy with which to approach poverty and destitution.

'Pauperism, in so far as sustained on the principle that each man, simply because he exists, holds a right on other men or on society for existence, is a thing not to be regulated but destroyed. Any attempt to amend the system which reposes on such a basis will present us with but another modification of that which is radically and essentially evil. Whatever the calls be which the poverty of a human being may have on the compassion of his fellows—it has no claims whatever upon their justice. . . . The proper remedy, or remedy of nature, for the wretchedness of the few, is the kindness of the many.'[7] Voluntary charity, of course, like a legal provision for the poor, was open to the objection that it merely distributed existing wealth without increasing its amount; but Chalmers believed that it would be more likely to be wisely directed, and less likely than a compulsory assessment to be excessive in amount and to encourage extravagant hopes in the poor.

Chalmers also held the firm conviction that men in general could be trusted to relieve of their own free-will such cases of need as were brought under their notice, and in that connexion he relied on four agencies: the self-help of the poor themselves who would be stirred to fend for themselves, if the demoralizing influence of doles were done away with; the help of relatives whose hearts and pockets would be opened when they saw their kin in need; the kindness of neighbours, who would make up by the number of their contributions for the smallness of each individual amount; and the charity of the well-to-do, which he considered least important. 'All which the rich give to the poor in private beneficence is but a mite and a trifle when compared with what the poor give to one another.'[8]

Local, unobserved, and unofficial charity was to Chalmers the ideal method of dealing with pauperism. Even in the case of illegitimate children and families deserted by the father Chalmers wished no parochial relief to be given. He held that family, friends, and private benevolence would do all that was needful, and that the knowledge that the burden would fall there, and not on public funds, would tend to diminish such cases. Any poor-relief system that was public, legal, centralized and therefore capable of indefinite augmentation was to be considered as mischievous, because it discouraged all the four agencies just mentioned, and so tended to create distress faster than it could relieve it. To try to cure poverty by a compulsory legal charity seemed like an attempt to quench a fire by pouring oil on the flames. It did not create, but merely distributed existing wealth and it was calculated to destroy the moral check, 'and so to call forth an augmented population, without the benefit of any augmented produce by which to meet the new demands itself had created.'[9]

In support of these opinions Chalmers could point to England where in the early decades of the nineteenth century there was an obvious social evil resulting from the Poor Law. The Speenhamland system of supplementing low wages out of the rates, on a scale related to the size of the labourer's family and to the price of bread, seemed a direct encouragement to the increase of population. While it may have served its immediate purpose of preventing distress from provoking violence, it proved disastrous to the self-respect and self-help of the rural working class of southern England.

Chalmers believed in breaking down the huge unmanageable task of coping with an industrialized Scotland into manageable portions by what he called the Principle of Locality. What he proposed was essentially the extension and adaptation of the system of the rural parish to the towns and cities. In a letter to Wilberforce in 1820 he wrote, 'nothing but the multiplication of our Established Churches with the subdivision of parishes and the allocation to each parish of its own church, together with a pure and popular exercise of the right of patronage, will ever bring us back again to a sound and wholesome state of the body politic.'[10] In order to demonstrate how irreligion, demoralization, and poverty could be overcome in this way Chalmers persuaded the City Fathers of Glasgow to erect a new parish, St. John's, with a population of some ten thousand persons, to which he was presented in 1819. There he made his great experiment, of which the poor-relief scheme was only one part, though the part by which the whole was judged.[11]

At that time in Glasgow there were two central bodies dealing with the poor. There was the Town Hospital, an administrative body which provided indoor and outdoor relief out of the funds raised by the compulsory assessment for the poor, and there was the General Session which gathered in the voluntary collections made at the doors of the parish churches and returned to the several kirk-sessions the sum needed for the cases on their poor-roll. Chalmers undertook to send no more paupers from the parish of St. John's to the Town Hospital, if the General Session would hand over to the kirk-session of his parish the sole control of the church door collections of St. John's.

To begin with Chalmers divided his large parish into twenty-five 'proportions' or subdivisions, each containing about four hundred persons—say sixty to one hundred households—a number not too large for a zealous church-worker to make effective contact with, so as to know the circumstances of every household. To each subdivision an elder was assigned, whose charge was the spiritual oversight of all the people, except such as were effectively connected with some dissenting church. In each 'proportion' there was a Sabbath School—perhaps more than one—staffed by voluntary teachers, who sometimes also conducted sewing classes for the girls. Further, there were day schools in the parish where, within reach of all, the Church provided education by competent teachers—an education cheap but not free, for Chalmers believed that people valued more highly what they had to make an effort to obtain. In these schools he contemplated the children of the well-to-do associating with the children of the poor, as had long been the case in the rural schools of Scotland. Thus would arise an evangelical democracy —not in the sense that distinctions of rank, class, and wealth would be abolished, but in the sense that there would be understanding and reciprocity of feeling between the classes. Finally, to each 'proportion' of the parish there was assigned a deacon, whose duty it was to look into the material needs of the people with a view to distinguishing between the deserving and the undeserving poor. If confronted with an application for help the deacon would see if anything could be done to get the applicant suitable employment and if relatives and neighbours might afford help, also whether the applicant's need was for a regular allowance or merely temporary help. Only when every alternative was exhausted should the deacon recommend to the Deacons' Court that the applicant be placed on the roll for a regular allowance. Thus through close investigation impostors would be unmasked and only the incapacitated and deserving poor be left for support out of the funds provided by church collections.[12]

The experiment made an encouraging start. The collections at the evening service, attended chiefly by parishioners, amounted to about £80 a year. This was left in the hands of the deacons, and with it they were to meet any new cases of pauperism arising in the parish. Having such a moderate sum at their command they would not be tempted to yield to the human failing of generosity with other people's money. The collections at the morning and afternoon services, which were attended by people from wealthier quarters of the city drawn by the fame of the preacher, amounted to about £400 a year, and this was retained by the kirk-session to meet the needs of the poor already on the roll. When the experiment began this burden amounted to no more than £225, and the balance of £175 was intended to provide against the uncertainties of the future. The immediate result surpassed the expectations of everyone, Chalmers himself included. The deacons found their £80 sufficient for new cases, and the kirk-session was able in the second year to relieve the Town Hospital of all the St. John's pauperism remaining on the funds provided by assessment besides endowing a parish school and paying salaries to three additional teachers.[13]

The results of this experiment in St. John's have afforded scope for controversy. Chalmers certainly inspired a vast amount of personal service and voluntary association in all manner of good works, showing what the Church could do for society when skilfully organized and enthusiastically led. The schools were an undoubted success, though even there criticism alleged that success attracted pupils from beyond the parish and, more serious, that the fees, small as they were, excluded the very poorest who were in most need of education. As regards poor-relief the criticisms were more pointed. Though Chalmers left Glasgow for a professorship at St. Andrews in 1823, four years after its inception, the experiment seemed at first to continue on its successful way. Not till 1837, by which time it had continued for eighteen years, did it come to an end with the inclusion of St. John's parish in the general scheme of the city's poor-relief. Despite the opposition which it met with in many quarters, Chalmers himself remained an unhesitating believer in his scheme and maintained that it had never had a fair chance, for two of his stipulations had not been carried out. There was no law of residence to prevent paupers from elsewhere settling in St. John's, and, more important, the parishioners of St. John's, besides bearing the cost of their own pauperism by voluntary collection, were still assessed for poor-rates like the inhabitants of the other city parishes.[14]

Among criticisms directed against the scheme was the charge that the methods of Chalmers tended rather to conceal than to relieve poverty, for everything depended on the attention, judgment and humanity of the deacons. Further, there was no provision for destitution resulting not from any moral fault but from trade depression. Again, the sharp discrimination between deserving and undeserving poor was designed, as his critic Dr. W. P. Alison pointed out, quoting Chalmers's own words, to let the undeserving 'feel the weight of those severities which are intended by the God of Nature to follow in the train of idleness, improvidence and vice'.[15] Was there not an undue moral rigour here out of harmony with the compassion which should mark a man, let alone a Christian? Chalmers claimed that his success was not due to his poor having migrated to other parishes: on the contrary St. John's suffered an accession of poor from elsewhere. While his good faith is not in doubt, it may be questioned whether his statistics fully covered the point at issue. He knew of the movements of those who were admitted to the poor-roll; but had he any means of knowing of those who may have moved to other parishes because they had no hope of obtaining relief in St. John's?

The experiment was perhaps successful enough to prove that, given certain conditions, this method of coping with poverty would succeed. Among these conditions—though Chalmers himself denied it—would seem to be the presence in every parish of a Chalmers to evoke the needful charity and to inspire the band of devoted workers to administer both it and the other parish agencies. At any rate, if there had ever been a chance of the St. John's scheme becoming general throughout Scotland, that chance was finally removed by the Disruption which gave conclusive point to the trend toward a secular and compulsory system of poor-relief.

It ought to be added, in justice to Chalmers, that while he hoped that the example of St. John's would be followed everywhere, and that the legal right of maintenance with the compulsory assessment accompanying it in many parishes would in time disappear in favour of the older Scottish method of poor-relief out of voluntary funds, he had no desire to hasten these changes at the cost of chaos and suffering. Thus, at the General Assembly of 1824, he actually seconded a motion that the Church should petition against a Bill for the abolition of poor-rates. Much as he desired that end, he wished the change to be gradual and at first to be permissive and not enforced by law.[16]

If a word had to be chosen to describe Chalmers's social ideal, perhaps 'paternalism' would come nearest to it. It was as we have seen a rural and conservative ideal, derived from the farm-house, the farm labourer's cottage, and the parish kirk—an ideal, therefore, with an increasingly old-world flavour in nineteenth-century Scotland. The best features of it were being undermined in the industrial areas by current social developments. The transformation of a rural peasantry into a city proletariat threatened the old independence and family loyalty of the people: the segregation of classes in the big cities and towns broke the close personal contacts of masters and servants which in a rural setting had mitigated the acuteness of social distinctions: and the increasing adoption of the system of compulsory assessment for the poor threatened the wholesome place of the Church in society as the dispenser of the charitable gifts of the faithful for the relief of the distressed. The old paternal order was passing away; but Chalmers believed that it could be restored and maintained, in essentials, even in the new industrial age, if only the Church, pulsing with evangelical zeal, could set its house in order, divide its old parishes into smaller, more manageable parishes, take the central place in every parish in the land, and by its ministers, teachers, elders, deacons, and other workers bring personal contact, spiritual, and moral teaching, and, in case of need, financial help to the whole population.

That this was no idle dream was proved in Glasgow by Chalmers himself in the Tron and St. John's parishes, and it was on the way to being proved in Edinburgh by Thomas Guthrie when the Disruption came and interrupted him. He came from Arbirlot to Old Greyfriars in 1837 with the intention of doing in Edinburgh what Chalmers had set forth in his *Christian and Civic Economy of our Large Towns*. Out of Old Greyfriars parish the new St. John's parish was formed, and St. John's church was opened in 1840. The gallery was let to applicants from any part of the city, but six hundred and fifty sittings, the whole area of the building, were reserved for free seats for residents in the parish, rich or poor, who applied for them. In his address at the opening of the church Guthrie said: 'We wish from its ruins to rebuild the ancient economy, and to restore what is not to be found nowadays in any burgh in all broad Scotland, a manageable parish, split up into districts, each containing ten or twenty families, with a free gospel in its parish church, with a school where the children of the poorest may receive at least a Bible education, and with its minister, its elders and its deacons, each in the active discharge of the duties of his own department.'[17]

It was in the ranks of the prospering middle classes that Chalmers found his zealous supporters and workers. He challenged his congregations with the needs of the depressed masses of the city and inspired in them evangelical enthusiasm, Christian compassion and also social alarm. It was a challenge which evoked a warm response from many of the younger men among his hearers—men like William Collins and David Stow. Stow, one of the most notable of Chalmers's young men, said, 'Till Dr. Chalmers came to Glasgow, parochial Christian influence was a mere name,—it was not systematic, it was not understood— there was not the machinery for the moral elevation of a town population. The people were let alone. Some of the elders of the Tron Church were excellent men, but their chief duty was to stand at the plate, receive the free-will offerings of the congregation as they entered, and distribute them to the poor by a monthly allowance. Their spiritual duties and exertions were but small, and almost exclusively confined to a few of the sick.'[18]

Soon after Chalmers came to the Tron, Sabbath evening schools were begun among the children of the poorest in the parish, and within two years, mainly under the direction of William Collins, upwards of twelve hundred children were under regular religious instruction in many small schools, the Bible and the Shorter Catechism being the text-books. The parish was divided into forty sections with thirty or forty houses in each. In some cases a single close was a section. Teachers were appointed for each section, and thus a territorial system of visitation and teaching came into being. It was from the success of this work that Chalmers conceived his scheme of territorial parish churches as the solution of the problem of industrial Scotland; and it was in such a Sabbath School that David Stow learned the ways of children and formulated principles which were to issue in a theory of the art of education and in professional training of teachers. Nevertheless, while Chalmers inspired a notable zeal for social improvement in many of the middle class in nineteenth-century Scotland, it may be surmised that others, neglecting his example and concentrating on his economic teachings, derived from them a positive discouragement to active effort for social betterment. If an increase of wages among the working classes was likely, in the absence of adequate moral restraint on their part, to lead to an increase of numbers so that the last state is worse than the first, the inference is ready to hand that the lower orders have chiefly themselves to blame for their condition and that unless they help themselves, little can be done by others that will permanently help them. Thus responsibility for the state of the poor is lifted from the external ordering of society, and particularly from the shoulders of persons of wealth and influence who occupy positions of prominence and leadership in the community; indeed the conviction is fostered that the socially superior must by that very fact be esteemed to be morally superior—a complex of doctrines congenial to the natural inertia of comfortable folk and to the moralistic stress which ever tends to pervert the thinking of the earnestly religious.

What can be said of the influence of Chalmers on the Scottish working classes? It may be doubted if he fully understood the new industrial population. He could probably understand the more capable, fortunate or energetic working man who might aspire to middle-class status as owner of a small business: he might even understand the demoralized victim of misfortune or vice; but had his experience given him the sympathy to understand the industrial working man, say in the cotton-spinning factory? His early experience in small centres of population inclined him to take a simple view of the relations of master and man, stressing their community of interest and their reciprocal duties. Perhaps he did not appreciate the new situation confronting men working in large factories under machine-production conditions and exposed to the stresses of booms and slumps. Moreover, his background of Adam Smith–Malthus economics, while it made him favourable to the repeal of the anti-combination laws, also made him doubt the value of trade unions and unfriendly to their claims. Since he held that the rate of wages was necessarily regulated by the supply of labour in proportion to the demand, he had no faith in the ability of the unions to raise wages above the natural level, nor, be it added, in the ability of governments or capitalists to depress wages below the market price.[19] Though he advocated complete liberty for workmen to form unions, he was well aware of the selfish, intolerant, and monopolistic spirit that often coloured their practice, and he wanted severe laws against intimidation. His economic theories and his conservative instincts combined to make him distrust the use which working men, organized under a group loyalty, would make of their corporate strength. Moreover, while there was something to be said for his campaign against legal assessments for poor-relief, it was not likely to carry conviction to working people confronted with actual cases of destitution at close quarters, and it was certain to raise doubts in their minds as to the genuineness of the humane and Christian principles of this outstanding churchman.

It is tempting to conjecture what might have been the effect on the Scottish working class if Chalmers had been able to associate himself, as Patrick Brewster did, with their aspirations. All that can certainly be said is that Chalmers's social message, admirable for stirring benevolence and service in the middle classes and for encouraging the working man to seek to rise in the world, was limited in its appeal to the self-conscious groups among the industrial working classes by its old-world rural paternalism and, still more, by its obsessive Malthusianism, and neglect of the economic and environmental factors in the situation.

As an economist Chalmers took the typical Scottish point of

view in that he treated economics as but one aspect of basic social policy. His great merits are the fundamental union of economic with religious and moral ideas and his insistence, as apt for our day as for his, that the supremely important thing for the well-being of society is the character of the individuals of whom it is composed. Further, while he may have been over-much influenced by the conditions of his early years, he cannot be blamed for not foreseeing the changes which the latter part of the nineteenth century was to bring; and he had certain economic insights which are relevant to our own times—the dependence of the capitalist on the antecedent ability of his customers to purchase his products and, therefore, the precedence which the interest of the consumer should take over that of the producer.[20]

From the vantage point of the present day two shortcomings in Chalmers as a social thinker fall to be noticed. One serious fault is his undue deference to Malthus. He shared the opinion of Adam Smith that free trade in corn would not seriously affect agricultural interests, for he supposed that owing to the high cost of transport Britain must continue to be largely self-supporting as regards food. This assumption of self-dependence joined to the rapid growth of population in his day made the theory of Malthus come home to him as self-evident truth. He stated that 'in spite of all the ridicule, and of all the sentimental indignancy which have been heaped on the doctrine of population, it remains as unalterable as any of nature's laws, that nothing can avail for the conducting of our peasantry to a higher status, but a lessened competition for employment, and in virtue of there being somewhat fewer labourers'.[21] The Malthusian cloud overshadowed Chalmers all the way. His heart urged him to desire the material prosperity as well as the moral and spiritual elevation of the people, but his mind, enthralled by Malthus, was too well aware of the limitations and dangers inherent in the obvious ways of approaching that goal. He could see no way except 'a more advantageous proportion between the food of the country and the number of its inhabitants; and no other way of securing this proportion than by the growth of prudence and principle among themselves'.[22] The doctrine of Malthus is in greater favour to-day than it has been for several generations. Many would agree that at certain epochs and in certain regions it points to the dominating factor in the social situation. They would deny, however, that that factor is so all-pervasive and commanding as Chalmers took it to be. Hence we must regret that he allowed it to condition his economic views and limit the impulses of his Christian heart. Again, from the point of view of the modern social scientist the fatal distortion in the outlook of Chalmers was that, in his zeal to abolish pauperism and prevent the demoralization of the masses, he ignored the social or non-individual factors in the poverty around him. We realize now that that poverty in its broad range was rooted in defective social and economic organization. It should be remembered, however, that there was not available to Chalmers anything like a scientific investigation into the facts of poverty such as the classical survey of London by Charles Booth two generations later. He had to rely on his own observation and it was intensive only during the eight years of his Glasgow ministry. Moreover the effects of contemporary bad housing and drinking customs were so serious and so obvious in his day that he may well be excused for extending the scope of moral factors unduly and holding that the poverty of the masses was rooted in individual moral shortcoming.

In the absence of an objective survey of the facts the situation almost inevitably became over-simplified. The unemployed, the under-nourished, the frustrated sought relief in drink or crime or other forms of depravity, thus giving plausibility to the opinion that poverty is the result of character weakness. Again, parents, giving up the struggle against over-crowding, disease and squalor, became irresponsible, and the children showed the consequences in vice and crime; still further confirming the view that the fault lies with the individual and that the remedy lies in religious and moral education. In those days it was more likely to be the medical man rather than the moralist or Christian minister who would give due weight to the environmental factors. For instance, W. P. Alison, the most significant opponent of Chalmers on the matter of the poor, held that while it might be possible to excite religious feelings in the lowest members of society, experience proved that such religion could not be expected to regulate their characters while they had to struggle for their existence. 'A certain degree of physical comfort is essential to the permanent development and habitual influence over human conduct of any feelings higher than our sensual appetites.'[23]

The influence of Chalmers on later thought and practice has been far-reaching. Of all the schemes influenced by his teaching and example the one most like his own was the Elberfeld system of poor-relief, so called from the town of Elberfeld in Rhenish Prussia but copied in many other towns in Germany during the later nineteenth century, and generally held to have been successful in normal times. Its origins go back to the beginning of the century, if not indeed to Hamburg in 1788.[24] In its mature form as operated in Elberfeld from 1853 it went on the principle that for every four recipients of aid there should be an unpaid visitor who, seeing the homes once a fortnight, would not only keep the town authorities acquainted with the circumstances of each case, but would also help with personal influence and advice. The methods of the system were disciplinary and educational as well as charitable, for its aim was to prevent pauperism altogether rather than to relieve hard cases. In the case of the incapacitated, if family and friends could not meet the need, relief was given out of public funds to bring the applicant's income up to a standard rate, varying from time to time but calculated to provide the basic necessities of life. In the case of the able-bodied relief was given in return for such work suited to their capacity as might be demanded of them. 'The scheme differed in many ways from that of Chalmers, yet there were important likenesses in the sub-division of the town under personal voluntary visitors, the care in choosing the visitors for their competence and kindliness, the careful inquiry and investigation of each case, the regular supervision and friendly advice, and in the use of what Chalmers called "the natural" resources of family and neighbourhood.'[25] The Elberfeld system reacted on English social work, for the Charity Organization Society owed some of its inspiration to what its Secretary, Charles Loch, saw at Elberfeld, while William Rathbone's work at Liverpool was influenced by what he, too, had learnt in Germany.

Chalmers in fact, both directly and indirectly, started a school of thought which issued in the Charity Organization Society movement with its distinctive technique of social work. This Society was founded in London in 1869 and a quarter of a century later no fewer than eighty-five organizations in various towns had embraced its principles.[26] Its outlook resembled that of Chalmers except in two particulars. While he wished state relief of poverty to be abolished, the Society recognized the need for a poor-law to relieve complete destitution, and while he set his deacons to visit from house to house, it preferred to visit only when asked and to see friends and relatives only with the client's consent.[27] Recent writers sum up the main contribution of Chalmers to this type of thought under five heads. First, he divided up a large urban area into small sections so that the voluntary worker could have personal knowledge of the poor and their circumstances. In this respect his example has been largely followed. Second, he taught the evil of promiscuous and sentimental giving and so anticipated by many decades the arguments of Charles Loch and his associates in the Charity Organization Society. Third, he pleaded for real understanding of all applications for relief, even at the cost of time and trouble on the part of the investigator. Fourth, he proclaimed the necessity of exhausting all possible sources of help before resorting to public funds. Fifth, he gave some attention to the selection and training of his workers. 'Nearly a century before organized formalized training began, Chalmers was thinking out what would be the best kind of people to supervise the districts and what advice on principle and method he could give them.'[28]

For a generation or more the C.O.S. approach has been under a cloud, while the philosophy of social welfare associated with the Webbs and the supporters of the 1909 Minority Poor-Law Report has enjoyed the sunshine of popular favour. Recently, however, signs of a reaction in opinion have begun to appear. Something is now being said in favour of fruitful co-operation between the statutory machinery of the social services and the voluntary societies. The work of Chalmers in Glasgow and its connexion with the C.O.S. movement has been studied in recent times, and it appears that, if we set aside his two serious errors mentioned above, much of his example is still relevant. The Stevenson Lecturer in Citizenship in Glasgow University has said, 'He insisted on the need for careful selection and training of social workers: on always working on a small scale, at the personal level: on making a careful study of each individual case: on keeping the family together. These are now the basic principles of modern social and family welfare.'[29]

The fact that Societies of Social Service—the modern name for the C.O.S.—continue to be active seems to suggest that, despite the increasing interest of the State in the welfare of its citizens, there are still many people in many kinds of trouble who do not find that the statutory provision meets their peculiar need. That need, if we may judge from the recent experience of such societies, is not primarily financial, though that element enters in to some extent. The financial help which such societies can give is not, and is not intended to be, a substitute for the help provided by the State. It is what they can give along with the financial help that is their main contribution. In that respect their work shows no sign of ceasing; and thus it would seem that Chalmers was right in thinking that family and social welfare demanded much more than augmented financial aid to the poor. So long as family case-work continues on the lines of the old Charity Organization Society, whatever be the name or auspices under which it is done, the teaching of Thomas Chalmers and its practice in Glasgow for eighteen years will not lack interest or relevance.

5

THE SCOTTISH CHURCH AND THE POOR

THE earliest Acts of the Scottish Parliament with reference to the poor seem to have been directed rather to repressing vagrants and idle beggars than to making provision for the destitute. The only class allowed to beg is defined in an Act of 1503 as 'crukit folk, blind folk, impotent folk and waik folk'.[1] The attitude of the Reformed Kirk is laid down in the *First Book of Discipline* which proposed that the poor should be a charge on the patrimony of the Kirk, declared that every kirk must provide for the poor within itself, and distinguished between 'the stout and strong beggar', who must be compelled to work, and the genuine poor who cannot work for a living.[2] In line with this we find a parliamentary statute of 1574 which provides for the punishment of strong and idle beggars and the sustentation of the poor and impotent, for which sustentation an assessment may be levied.[3] Acts on the subject were frequent during the next hundred years, the most important being the Act of 1672 which remained the basis of the Scottish poor-law until 1845. Thereafter the legal position was that the care of the aged and impotent poor was entrusted to the heritors and kirk-session in every parish. Legal assessments might be imposed. Sturdy beggars were provided for in two ways. Either they could be seized and set to work by manufacturers, coal-masters, and salt-masters for eleven years or they could be sent to 'houses of correction', which might be described as parish factories.[4] It must be added, however, that the system as set forth in the Acts of Parliament was much modified in practice. The correction-houses failed altogether to materialize, and for many generations few parishes adopted the practice of compulsory assessment.

The main source of income for relief under the Scottish system for the management of the poor during the eighteenth century and the early decades of the nineteenth was church collections. These were supplemented by gifts, mortifications, fines and fees of several sorts. Compulsory assessments were sanctioned by law, but were little used until the nineteenth century. Prior to 1700 there were but three parishes assessed: before 1740 probably not more than eight. Between 1700 and 1800 there were added ninety-three. In 1818 there were one hundred and forty-five. In landward parishes half the assessment was paid by heritors and half by tenants. In burghs the assessment was laid on all the inhabitants, or at least on all who seemed able to pay.[5]

Except in a very few cases such as friendless lunatics and foundlings, the relief given was admittedly supplementary to relief from other sources such as the charity of relatives and licensed begging within the parish. As the Assembly Report of 1839 put it—'a small sum given to aid their other resources affords them the relief which is necessary: and it would be against the true interests and the moral habits of the people if a more ample provision were made for them by their parishes'.

Settlement was never the difficult and contentious question in Scotland that it was in England. The period of continuous residence necessary for a person to acquire a settlement was three years, and there was no power of removal on the ground that a person was likely to become chargeable. Indeed the 1818 Report of the General Assembly goes so far as to say that 'it does not appear that there ever has been one instance of the removal of a pauper from one parish to another involuntarily or by legal means'. It appears, however, that means were frequently found of inducing persons who became destitute without having acquired a legal settlement to return to their native parishes.[6]

The able-bodied poor were not recognized by law at all, and denial of relief to them was fundamental to the system. Nevertheless there were periods of emergency when distress was acute and special measures had to be taken. The 1818 Report of the General Assembly, under the heading, 'relief to the industrious poor in 1817-18' referred to 'the extent of the distress felt in the above years throughout the whole of Scotland' and to the 'humane and liberal exertions made by the heritors and opulent inhabitants to relieve it'.

The relief of the poor rested in the hands of the kirk-session, supported by the heritors in country parishes and by the magistrates in the burghs. Two classes of poor were admitted—the ordinary or infirm poor, who received allowances as a legal right, their names being placed on the poor-roll, and the occasional poor who were temporarily in need owing to illness or accident and had their allowances at discretion and not by right. Use and wont decreed that one half of the church collections should be used for the occasional poor. Moreover the kirk-session had under its own control such sources of income as fines and fees, the heritors having no part in these. Less regular or reputable methods were sometimes used. The 1818 Report said: 'In most parts of Scotland extraordinary collections for the relief of individual distress or misfortune are not uncommon . . . it is a still more usual practice to have recourse in such cases to private contributions than to public collections. Sometimes a Session grants a certificate of the facts; and the distressed individual (or some of his friends) takes it, with an accompanying petition, to the wealthy inhabitants of the parish. . . . Sometimes a raffle is made of some article he can most conveniently spare; and sometimes balls or other public meetings of amusement are held, and the surplus profits are applied for his benefit. . . . Nor should it be omitted to notice here the commendable custom followed in several parishes, of a number of young persons in a body uniting to solicit the inhabitants at Christmas or on New Year's Day and to make a collection for the benefit of the poor, which they afterwards distribute themselves.'[7]

In practice the heritors seldom or never interfered in regulating the concerns of the poor or of the poors' fund, except in assessment parishes,[8] and even in these parishes they did not interfere with the occasional relief. The elders were the almoners as well as the overseers, but in some parishes one of them, as treasurer, distributed the allowances at stated times and places.

There seems to have been an understanding at one time that the Sheriff might revise the findings of a kirk-session, for the General Assembly's Committee in 1818 mentions twenty-six cases, mostly in assessment parishes in the Borders, where the Sheriff on appeal fixed a higher allowance than the Session proposed. The very next year, however, the Court of Session put an end to this practice. In 1819 during a period of great distress in Paisley numbers of the unemployed applied for parish relief and were refused on the ground that being able-bodied, they were not 'within the class of poor for which the law provided'. The Sheriff ordered an assessment for the purpose; but on appeal

the supreme court ruled that 'first, whether claimants of parochial aid are of the description of persons that are entitled to such
relief: and secondly, if they be of this description of persons,
what shall be the amount of the assessment and relief—is vested
in the heritors and kirk-session of the parish, and no control of
the proceedings and determination of the kirk-session in these
particulars is committed to sheriffs or other inferior judicatures'.[9]
This meant that the only appeal lay to the Court of Session itself,
and, in view of the expense involved, that was little better than
no appeal at all.

There seems to have been an understanding that dissenters
from the Established Church would look after their own occasional poor, though with the ordinary poor the legal obligation
was admitted whatever the religion of the applicant. Practice,
however, seems to have varied, for the General Assembly stated:
'In many parishes all the poor of the dissenters are on the poors'
roll: in others they are partially relieved. . . . Some classes of
the dissenters support their own poor: others contribute to the
parish funds by occasional collections or a stated annual sum
paid, but in most cases they do not contribute to them at all.'[10]

Underlying the system there were three guiding principles:
the denial of relief to the able-bodied, whether in or out of an
institution; the absence of any central control, as each parish,
subject to a theoretical right of appeal to the supreme court,
could go its own way; and, according to the 1844 Report, outdoor relief which was the essence of the scheme. There were
some ancient hospitals and a few almshouses and houses of
refuge; but there were no poorhouses in the later sense, and institutions of any kind were quite exceptional. 'We may sum up
by saying that before 1845 there was a statutory and elaborate
system of poor relief, including a local administrative authority
—though without any responsible central authority—a compulsory assessment, a law of settlement and prohibition of relief to
the able-bodied.'[11]

The part of the Church, both as ordained by law and in actual
practice, was central, for the whole system was administered on a
parochial basis by minister and kirk-session. Though the *First
Book of Discipline*'s scheme for making the support of the poor
a charge on the patrimony of the Kirk failed to find legal enact-
ment, nevertheless the Scottish poor-law remained closely

linked with the Church Establishment, and its guiding principles are in line with the social views set forth in the *First Book
of Discipline*. It was assumed that a clear distinction could be
drawn between the deserving and the undeserving poor. That
distinction can be traced in the early Acts of the Scottish Parliament; but it comes to clear statement in the *First Book of Discipline*, where the deserving poor are described as 'the widow
and fatherless, the aged, impotent or lamed' also 'persons of
honesty fallen into decay and penury', while the undeserving
poor appear as 'stubborn and idle beggars, who, running from
place to place, make a craft of their begging'. For the deserving
it is claimed that 'reasonable provision must be made for their
sustentation', but that is not further defined either in the *Book
of Discipline* or in the Act of Parliament of 1574 which speaks of
'needful sustentation'.[12]

In the rural parishes there were few complexities. The kirk-
session was concerned with morality and discipline as well as
poor relief. Minister and elders would have an intimate knowledge of the situation and character of the parties concerned, and
could treat the poor as persons rather than as cases, though
doubtless there was opportunity also for petty tyranny. Sometimes a special collection would be made for hard cases. In 1761
a widow in Auchterless who had a young family to support lost
her cow a few days before calving. The cow was almost her sole
means of subsistence. The Session ordered a collection and the
minister represented the sad circumstances to the congregation
with the result that five times the ordinary amount of the church
collection was received.[13] For others measures might be taken by
a Session which at the present day would be held to fall within
the sphere of the public health authorities. For example, from
1758 down to the early decades of the nineteenth century one
finds kirk-sessions in Aberdeenshire sending young women to
Aberdeen and paying their fees in order that they might be
trained in midwifery by doctors there and return to their parishes
to practise their art.[14] Again, the difficulty of securing a woman
to attend the helpless poor was so great at Methlick in 1801
that the Session built an apartment for an aged pauper beside
the house of the person who was found willing to give attendance.[15]

In the towns, too, the actual management was in the hands

of the kirk-session, but in crowded city parishes the personal touch grew less and less. Moreover, towards the end of the eighteenth century and in the early years of the nineteenth the traditional assumptions became less applicable to the poverty that showed itself in the industrial areas. A factory might close down, a whole trade might experience a period of depression, and the victims might be upright and industrious persons. Genuine unemployment, reflecting no discredit on the people concerned, appeared on the scene. On the other hand conditions began to emerge in the cities which seemed to give strong confirmation to the moral assumptions underlying the existing system of dealing with the poor. In city slums were gathered masses of poor folk, many unquestionably undeserving—drunken, vicious, and criminal. Some might suggest that it was poverty and frustration that drove them to their evil ways, but to most observers it seemed clear that their poverty was the result of moral failings. Nevertheless something had to be done for them for, if left alone, they might prove a menace to the stability of society. The Industrial Revolution was thus seriously complicating the whole problem of the poor and the methods of dealing with them. It is not surprising that when in the changed circumstances the line between deserving and undeserving poor could not be so clearly drawn, it was difficult for Christian people to adjust their attitude to those in distress.

The stage was being set, in fact, for the controversy on the management of the poor in Scotland which came to a head in the early forties and issued in the Act of 1845. That controversy turned on two related questions. Were the sums given in relief adequate? Was the voluntary system adequate or ought it to be replaced by a system of compulsory assessment? There can be no doubt that the relief given was totally inadequate for full maintenance. The prevalent scale of relief could only be justified on the understanding that it was to supplement what was contributed by neighbourly benevolence and public charity. There was, as the minister of Mauchline put it, 'ample ground for the common observation "that it is the poor in Scotland who maintain the poor". '[16] Stevenson Macgill reported that 'in the year 1815 the net average paid to the first class of poor in Glasgow who require the least regular aid was £1. 17s. per annum: the net average of the highest class who receive pensions was £2. 16s.

Those who are totally destitute, such as orphans or aged persons confined to bed, are received into the poors' house. . . .'[17] A generation later the figures seem to have advanced but little. Sheriff Alison reported: 'The amount of aliment which is generally awarded even in great towns such as Glasgow and Edinburgh is a shilling a week, or about three halfpence a day—a pittance upon which in large towns it is barely possible to support a suffering and lingering existence.'[18] Similarly the Rev. George Lewis, writing in 1841 said: 'the poor-roll of Dundee, in common with other large towns of Scotland, only informs us of the poverty relieved, and is silent as to the poverty *unrelieved*. The entire pensioners on the poor-roll of this town are only 1,178, having allowances, for themselves and families, of one or two shillings a week—a sum incapable of supporting any human being.'[19] According to W. P. Alison the largest allowance in the old town of Edinburgh was two shillings to two shillings and sixpence per week per family.

These quotations have brought us to our second question and have also indicated that some ministers in the industrial areas were being forced by facts to question the adequacy of the voluntary system. As early as 1819 Stevenson Macgill asserted that 'the law of assessment is then necessary in order to secure an adequate and steady relief to the poor under all the different and varying circumstances of places and countries'.[20] At the end of a thorough discussion of the subject he wrote: 'The conclusions which, according to my apprehension, should be formed on this subject are that Assessments, Collections, Charitable Societies for Special Purposes, and liberal and regular Private Charities, in their own place, and when wisely conducted, are all of the highest moment, and will be found, united, to do nothing more than is proper for the relief of our fellow-creatures; that so far from being opposed to one another they easily combine; that, under a wise system and management they are free from those evils of which they are accused. . . .'[21]

A review of Macgill's book in the *Edinburgh Christian Instructor* for 1820 referred particularly to his views on the poor and agreed with him that a legal provision in the shape of a compulsory assessment had become necessary. This opinion is all the more significant since the review was almost certainly written by the editor, Dr. Andrew Thomson of St. George's, Edinburgh, a man

of penetrating intellect as well as generous heart. He refers with
strong approval to Macgill's conclusion, and he has his own
pointed comments on the result of the assessment policy. 'It is
readily acknowledged', he wrote, 'that in general, whenever
assessments take place there is a considerable increase in the
numbers of the poor and in the expense of their maintenance.
But even here there is often a great deal of deception; and it
would be found, that neither the number of the poor is really
increased, nor the expense, but that the whole of the poor have
now become visible, many of whom had formerly been hid; and
that they come wholly or chiefly on the assessment for their
maintenance, instead of obtaining it in other ways. . . . It ought
not to be any cause of regret that those of the poor who were
starving in their houses, should come forward and apply for
their share of the assessment; nor that those who were supported
by the general funds of the country in the shape of begging,
should be put on the fund of their own parish. . . . We are certainly on the whole averse to assessments, if there were a possibility of making adequate provision for the poor without them.
. . . But matters are now come to that pass, in most places, that
there either must be assessments, or the poor must be left to
starve or beg, or be thrown as a burden on their poor relations.'[22]

Andrew Thomson's successor in the leadership of the rising
Evangelical party in the Church of Scotland, Thomas Chalmers,
took the opposite view. He maintained that if the poor knew that
there was a legal provision on which they could count when over-
taken by misfortune, they would become reckless and improvident and their numbers increase. 'It is impossible', he declared,
'but that an established system of pauperism must induce a great
relaxation on the frugality and providential habits of our labouring classes.'[23] His plan for dealing with the poor was to multiply
the religious and educational establishment of the cities and
towns many times over, so that the parishes there as in the rural
districts might become workable areas with a manageable population, where a vigorous and popular ministry would create and
control the agencies of moral uplift centred in the Church. 'We
hold it a practical thing to conduct any parish, either in the city
or in the country, to the old economy of a Scottish parish.'[24]
This application of rural parish methods to urban destitution
would result, he believed, in a revival in the new situation of the

old virtues and independence of the peasantry. Chalmers, in short, made explicit the assumptions of Scottish legislation and practice down the centuries—that, apart from 'acts of God', such as congenital deficiencies or accidents, which could be left to local charity, poverty was the result of faults of character, that the emphasis should be on prevention rather than relief, and that prevention should be through the agency of the educational and religious establishment. Chalmers proceeded to demonstrate his confidence in his own opinions by putting them to a practical test in St. John's Parish, Glasgow. The success of his experiment has been variously estimated. It was not successful in convincing his critics, especially Dr. W. P. Alison, Professor of Medicine in the University of Edinburgh, who, a year after the appearance of the 1839 Assembly Report, gave voice to a grave indictment of the Scottish system for the care of the poor.

Finding in his professional experience diseases which were obviously the result of privation, he was led, as he said, 'to extend his enquiries to the grand evil of Poverty itself, and endeavour to apply to it the same principles of investigation by which physicians are guided in determining the immediate causes and remedies of disease.'[25] His conclusions were that the increasing sufferings of the poor were much greater and more general in Scottish than in English towns of similar size; that the repeated epidemics of fever in these towns were in great measure the result and indication of previous misery and destitution; that the higher ranks in Scotland did much less, for the relief of poverty and the sufferings resulting from it, than those of any other well-regulated country in Europe; that the allowances granted to the poor were quite inadequate; and that towns where there were assessments proved a point of attraction to people from country parishes where there were none, thus throwing the burden of destitution and disease on the places where there was relief and medical provision.

While his approach was thus primarily empirical Alison did not hesitate also to take the highest ground, and to point out that to clothe the naked and feed the hungry was a religious duty distinctly enjoined in Scripture, and that those who made assertions tending to modify this obligation ought to justify them. Moreover, he denied that a fixed legal provision for the poor had produced the results claimed by Chalmers. Experience supported the contrary view 'that in a country advanced in civilization, population makes the most rapid progress where least is done for the poor; that its tendency (inherent in human nature) to outstrip the means of subsistence, is most effectually restrained where a fixed and uniform provision . . . is known to exist; and that no religious or moral education which can be given them, without the aid of such provision against destitution and misery, is effectual in teaching them prudence, or restraining their tendency to excessive increase'.[26]

Alison also affirmed that the system adopted in St. John's Parish, Glasgow, never gave regular and certain relief to all the destitution that existed there, but only to a part of it, and, surveying the whole country, he declared that 'the legal relief to destitution was most uncertain and irregular, and almost everywhere inadequate', and that what preserved great numbers of the poor from starvation was 'one form or other of mendicity'.[27] There was, moreover, no prospect of Chalmers's scheme being carried out over the whole country: the distinction between deserving and undeserving poor meant leaving to beggary those, together with their innocent children, whom the deacons might judge undeserving: and it made no provision for that destitution which results from unemployment—'a source of destitution which has now become, and, in all probability will henceforth continue, so frequent in Scotland as to demand imperatively some more permanent provision than has yet been made for it'.[28]

Alison denied that the parochial system, with the moral management which Chalmers recommended, was incompatible with the extension of the legal provision, as Chalmers thought; and among the practical advantages of the legal assessment system he advanced these—it was the only system of relief which, in a complex society, where great numbers of the rich and poor lived widely apart, could be truly effectual in preserving a large portion of the poor from misery and degradation; it was the only system which could be just to the lower and to the higher ranks of society, inasmuch as it spread the burden over both the charitable and the uncharitable; it was the only system which could operate uniformly in proportion to the wants and be adapted to the character of the sufferers; and it gave all ranks of the community a direct interest in the condition of the poor.[29]

Alison's immediate proposals for Scotland were: that the power to enforce existing statutes for adequate relief of all destitute persons, for whom they were designed, should be lodged with some impartial body, perhaps Sheriffs and magistrates, where it could be exercised without expense to the parties concerned; that assessments should be imposed uniformly throughout the country; that assessments and the allowances to widows and orphans, aged, disabled, and impotent folk should be much increased; that the workhouse system should be introduced into every considerable town, and unions of parishes formed in rural areas to maintain workhouses, with fever hospitals in connexion with the workhouses; that relief ought to be regularly given to those proved to be destitute for want of employment, and that this should be given, unless in very peculiar circumstances, in the workhouses only; and that the burden of poverty be equalized as much as possible by raising the residence qualification from three to seven or even ten years.[30]

W. P. Alison found a strong supporter in his brother Archibald Alison, Sheriff of Lanarkshire, whose volumes on *The Principles of Population* appeared in 1840. He examined the Malthusian bogey and dismissed it, declaring that 'no danger need ever be apprehended from measures which better the condition of the poor; it is from their degradation and suffering that a redundancy of numbers, from their comfort and prosperity that a due regulation of population is to be expected'.[31] The Sheriff had no doubt as to the origin of the poor of Edinburgh and Glasgow —'two-thirds of the poor of these great cities are composed of the rural paupers who have been driven into the towns by the almost total want of relief, either legal or voluntary, in the country'.[32] He made a generous plea for the operative workmen who, he surmised, shared least in the advantages of the wealth which their industry created, and said, 'the security of a provision in sickness or old age is nothing more than a fair compensation for the risks which they run and the contamination to which they are exposed: for health which is undermined, morals which are corrupted, foresight which is destroyed, sensuality which is disseminated.'[33] To the misery and destitution of the population the Sheriff ascribed the forty-fold increase in serious crime in Scotland between 1808 and 1838; and he suggested one simple and obvious remedy for some of the abuses of the poor-law. 'All that is necessary,' he said, 'is to give the ordinary local courts of law jurisdiction in questions between paupers and the heritors and kirk-sessions having the administration of the poor funds, both as to the persons admissible on the poors' roll, and the amount of aliment to be awarded. In the Small Debt Courts of the Sheriffs or Justices of the Peace cases of this sort might be decided in a week, and at a cost of a few shillings each. Such a change seems all that is necessary to put the present law on a most salutary footing.'[34]

The facts and arguments brought forward by W. P. Alison made a great impression and were greeted with enthusiasm by those who had come to similar conclusions. Patrick Brewster of Paisley in the third of the discourses which brought a libel upon him declared that Alison had 'undeniably proved also from extensive and accurate inquiry—what was indeed previously known to all who had turned their attention to the subject—that the parochial relief given in Scotland has long been totally inadequate'.[35] Thomas Carlyle, writing early in 1843, referred to 'the brave and humane Dr. Alison who speaks what he knows', and declared roundly, 'Scotland, too, till something better come, must have a Poor-Law, if Scotland is not to be a byword among the nations.'[36]

The Church as a whole was slow to realize the difference that the Industrial Revolution was making, though not quite so slow as some have supposed. At the time of the first Statistical Account in the 1790's few ministers supported the principle and practice of assessments on their own merits.

The venerable Dr. Samuel Charters of Wilton boldly declared that 'the minister of a populous parish, where there is no poorsrate, is distressed with the view of indigence, which he cannot relieve, and may be tempted to turn away his eye from beholding it; but under the benign influence of poor laws he can enter the abodes of the wretched, as the messenger of good tidings. The law which provides for the poor, instead of dissolving, tends to strengthen pastoral and parental and filial love.'[37] At the other end of the country, John Bethune of Dornoch, where the poor funds came from church collections and small fines, expressed the wish 'that by assessments upon heritors, tenants and others, in proportion to their several interests, holdings and circumstances, a certain provision were made for their subsistence'.[38]

From a survey of the first Statistical Account, however, Dr. Robert Burns of Paisley concluded that in the period 1792–8 the number of parishes in which assessments more or less obtained was ninety-two; that the general sense of the Church appeared to be in favour of the old method of providing for the poor by collections and voluntary subscriptions where there were no insuperable difficulties in the way: and that where assessments were approved of, it was principally on the plea of necessity—arising from the non-residence of heritors, their neglect of public worship and weekly collections, the increase of dissenters, the growth of manufactures with consequent influx of strangers, and other similar causes. Assessments were also vindicated on the ground of their tendency to equalize the burden of supporting the poor and to prevent the increase of mendicity.[39] In the first Statistical Account there is, in fact, little to indicate that the management of the poor was a problem. Life in the countryside in the eighteenth century for the mass of the population was hard and laborious, and if there is little recognition of the hardships of those who eked out an existence by begging and by grants from the parish poor box, that may be simply because they were not so much worse off than their neighbours. By 1819, however, as we have seen, several prominent Scottish churchmen in the cities, like Stevenson Macgill and Andrew Thomson, were definitely in favour of a legal assessment. On the other hand Robert Burns at that time agreed with the Interim-Report (1817) of the General Assembly's Committee as transmitted to Parliament 'that it appears to the Committee from the returns before them, that the weekly collections at the churches are a very efficient resource for the parochial poor, in every case in which there are few Dissenters, or persons who absent themselves from their parish church; it is equally clear, on the other hand, that in those parishes in which the accommodation provided for the inhabitants in the parish churches bears no proportion to the population, a legal assessment seems to be inevitable, as long as this continues to be the situation of those parishes'.[40] When the Committee sent in its full report in 1818 it expressed the 'decided conviction not only that the practice of legal and compulsory assessments for the support of the poor is radically unwise and dangerous, but also that the crisis has already arrived, when Scotland should in every quarter take the alarm and form precautions against the farther spread in our country of so baneful a national calamity'.[41]

Again in 1839, complying with a government request, the General Assembly prepared a report about the maintenance of the poor in Scotland. The principal circumstances calling for a change of policy were stated in this later report to be the increased difficulty of maintaining the poor by collections, due to the expanding population, particularly in the manufacturing districts, without a corresponding increase in the ecclesiastical establishment. On that account assessments had become inevitable in commercial and manufacturing areas such as the Barony parish of Glasgow. Nevertheless, though the number of assessed parishes had by 1839 risen to 236, the report still defended the voluntary system and spoke of the evils of assessment. By this time, however, Robert Burns, taught by his Paisley experience, was taking up a stronger attitude, akin in this matter to that of his fellow-minister and Presbytery opponent Patrick Brewster. He declared in 1841, 'The absolute failure . . . of even the best scheme of voluntary beneficence has rendered systematic plans of relief absolutely necessary.'[42]

By this time matters were coming to a head, for in 1841 the General Assembly was presented with a report from its Committee on Pauperism which, while strongly deprecating 'any departure from the two great principles of the Scottish system viz., that the legal provision for the poor is only in supplement of that flowing from charity, and that a legal right to relief should not be given to those whose destitution arises from want of employment, and not from disability to work', nevertheless recommended the Assembly 'to give their countenance and support to the demand for an inquiry', but on the understanding that certain conditions as to the qualifications of the commissioners and their terms of reference should be fulfilled.[43] This conclusion was reaffirmed by the General Assembly of 1842.

It was not simply the arguments of W. P. Alison and others which brought over public opinion to the view that a change was necessary. At least equally potent was the period of economic depression, affecting some important trades in particular, which set in after 1836 and led to acute distress in certain districts in the early 1840s. In Paisley, for instance, such a state was reached that relief funds were raised both in Scotland and in England

and the Government sent a commissioner to investigate the situation. His findings gave impetus to the growing demand for an inquiry into the general working of the Scottish poor-law system, and in 1843 a Commission of Inquiry was appointed.

If anything was needed to give urgency to the Commission's work it was the Disruption which finally extinguished the faint possibility that Dr. Chalmers's St. John's scheme might become generally operative throughout the country. The Commission condemned the existing system on two main counts: that there was scarcely any provision for the sick poor in most parts of the country, these unfortunate folk being left to the operations of private charity, frequently that of medical men; and that such poor relief as was available was generally uncertain and insufficient. The principal recommendations of the Commission were embodied in the Act of 1845 which created a statutory obligation to make provision for the sick poor and not only reaffirmed the duty of the parish to provide poor relief, but placed that duty under a measure of supervision. Relief, however, was still limited to the aged and infirm poor, no provision being made for able-bodied poor in times of depression. The parish remained the unit of administration; but there was established a central Board of Supervision with general responsibility for the relief of the poor, and under it parochial boards each with an inspector of poor as its agent. It lay with these local boards to decide whether or not their parishes were to be assessed. Sanction was given to the provision of poorhouses where parishes or unions of parishes had five thousand inhabitants, but such provision was not compulsory and there was no idea of using the poorhouse as a test. Its purpose was to accommodate aged and friendless impotent folk, including idiots and improvident persons unable to look after their own affairs. The local inspector of poor was criminally liable for the death of any person whose application for relief had been refused, and he was fortified against local pressure by being made dismissable only by the Board of Supervision. An applicant who had been refused relief could appeal to the Sheriff and if the relief granted seemed inadequate he could appeal to the Board of Supervision. Under these conditions it is not surprising that as time went on the assessment system was more widely adopted, the number of poorhouses increased and the average allowance to each pauper steadily mounted.

The Poor Law Amendment Act of 1845 must have been a disappointment to many, for it maintained most of the characteristic features of the traditional Scottish system, and the changes effected by it seem strangely meagre in view of the magnitude of the social problems of the day. On the general issue between the Poor Law reformers and their opponents there can be no doubt that the reformers were right. The Scottish system was inadequate and poverty was a main cause of the troubles of the times. On the other hand an Act of Parliament tending towards an augmented and more certain poor relief proved totally inadequate to cope with these troubles. Better housing, the diminution of drunkenness, the control of epidemic disease by sanitary reform—these were also urgent lines of attack on contemporary ills, and it may be, as a recent writer has suggested, that 'the Poor Law reform movement had perhaps one unfortunate result: by concentrating attention on one aspect of reform it may have served to slow down other necessary improvements'.[44]

The most radical change made by the Act of 1845 was that it took the responsibility for the care of the poor out of the hands of the Church. It must not be supposed, however, that the interest of Scottish churchmen in this matter ceased after 1845. Members of kirk-sessions continued to form part of the parochial boards for nearly half a century. There were sufficient anomalies and problems still remaining to keep criticism of the Act and its administration a recurrent phenomenon, all the more so since the Chalmers tradition remained strong in men like Hugh Miller, who claimed that the plans of Chalmers had never had a fair trial and yet realized that it was impossible to go back upon the Act of 1845.

How radical a change that Act made in one respect may be gathered from a statement of the General Assembly's Committee in 1818—'however difficult and laborious the duties are which the ministers and elders have to discharge in managing and distributing so large a sum (including the Session funds of the whole parishes of Scotland) as passes through their hands; yet all these duties have been performed from the Reformation to this day gratuitously; though by a moderate computation they employ regularly the active services of not less than four thousand individuals'.[45] That was no empty boast for, as we have seen, for many generations ministers and elders were both overseers and almoners of the poor and, in the course of their duties as such, contrived often, if not invariably, to deal with the poor as persons and to extend to them that sympathetic recognition of their place in the community without which charity or legal relief is cold and bare.

6

JOHN DUNLOP AND THE
SCOTTISH TEMPERANCE REFORMATION

D RUNKENNESS, largely caused by the consumption of spirits, was a great and growing evil in Scotland in the early decades of the nineteenth century. A century earlier, and indeed for centuries before that, the common beverages of Lowland Scotland had been French wines and home-brewed ale or beer. In the Highlands whisky was produced in unlicensed stills in the glens, but a witness could tell a Select Committee in 1834 that 'about fifty or sixty years ago, there were but few distilleries in Scotland; and if we go back as far as 1750, if I recollect right, there were only four or five at that time'.[1] In 1725 Walpole imposed a malt tax which met with furious opposition in Scotland. There were riots in Glasgow during which the military fired and a number of people were killed. This tax seems to have had much to do with the decline in the consumption of ale and the spread of a taste for smuggled foreign spirits and also for whisky which could be made illicitly more readily than ale. After the middle of the century and the opening up of the Highlands the consumption of whisky increased steadily throughout the country and tended to oust the consumption of less potent drinks.

In the eighteenth century liquor figured at all social occasions, and an inn near the church seemed a necessity so that worshippers might obtain both liquid and solid refreshment between the services; but about the middle of the century and for some time thereafter the lower classes drank little spirits and notorious drunkenness was confined to the upper ranks. Some shocking tales are on record of the length to which they carried their orgies of drinking.[2] As the second half of the century advanced, however, and especially when the French wars brought high wages and profits, the lower ranks began to ape the upper in matters of drink as in other respects, and the use of spirits increased. George Lewis, writing in 1841, summed up a long development in these terms: 'Fifty years ago hard drinking was the habit and boast of the upper classes—their distinction as men of property and family. From them this sin descended to the merchants, manufacturers and farmers of Scotland, who imitated but too faithfully the brutal habits of their superiors; and now this habit, disappearing from both upper and middle ranks, has descended amidst the working-classes and is devouring their earnings and making havoc of their family happiness and comfort.'[3]

The Old Statistical Account shows that as early as the 1790's parish ministers were becoming concerned about these tendencies. 'It is not twenty-five years ago,' said the account of Dunfermline, 'when almost nothing but the ale brewed in the town was drunk by the trades people.' Now, however, 'the general use of whisky is arrived at an alarming height among many of the lower ranks of life.'[4] Another account, after referring to a tolerably good inn and two respectable public houses in the village of Balfron, mentioned 'a great many low public houses, which deal only in whisky, and which are productive of the worst effects both to the health and morals of the people'.[5] Of Tranent it is recorded that 'at a moderate computation, betwixt 3,000 and 4,000 gallons of whisky are annually retailed in the parish, besides what are commissioned by private families from the stills. The extraordinary consumption of this article throughout Scotland at large may indicate a thriving trade and a productive revenue, but affords a small prospect of a sudden increase in moral and social virtues.'[6] Even more gloomy is the report from Kirkliston. 'It is utterly impossible that spirits can remain at their present price (about three shillings the English gallon in retail) without becoming the beverage of the common people.' The writer wishes the price of spirits to be raised, and concludes thus: 'the habit of drinking spirits will finally overcome every sentiment of honour and ambition in the human character.'[7]

The early decades of the nineteenth century brought changes in this already alarming situation, and these were nearly all for the worse. The evangelical revival, it is true, had some influence in making a moderate sobriety fashionable with some of the aristocracy and with a large section of the middle class; but the eighteenth-century tradition of heavy drinking having descended to the lowest ranks, the number of occasions with which the consumption of spirits was associated tended to increase. Moreover, strong liquors were becoming both cheaper and easier to obtain. Contemporary observers seem agreed that the fatal year was 1822, when the duty on spirits which stood at about 7 shillings the Scotch gallon was reduced to 2s. 10d. 'We thought,' said William Collins in 1834, 'that it would only be a short and sudden ebullition of drunkenness produced by the excitement of the spirit dealers' advertisements and the novelty of obtaining cheap whisky, but in that we were deceived.'[8] In 1820 the official figures for the consumption of spirits were about two million gallons; but by 1830 this had risen to nearly six million gallons. No doubt the steep fall in the duty had made smuggling less profitable, so that the official figures would be much nearer the actual consumption in 1830 than in 1820, but such a large increase cannot be ascribed to this alone, especially as the total consumption continued to increase—despite some decrease due to the influence of temperance societies after 1830—until by the middle of the century it was nearly seven million gallons, even though the duty had risen again by 1840 to 3s. 8d. a gallon.[9]

Along with this decline in price went a vast increase in facilities for acquiring drink. Down to 1794 general permits to retail wines and spirits cost between £4 and £7 according to the rent, and the total for the whole country was estimated at about one thousand, though there were also many irregular places where drink was obtainable. In 1794, however, cheap licences to retail whisky only were issued, and in a single year the number of establishments licensed to sell drink was increased almost five-fold. By 1824 there were 3,595 general licences and 7,539 whisky licences, in all more than 11,000. By 1830 the total had increased to over 17,000.[10] According to law magistrates had a right to refuse an application for a licence; but in practice they seldom did. The law gave them discretion as to the number and description of persons whom it might be 'meet and convenient' to license; but, as Sheriff-substitute Campbell of Renfrewshire complained to the Select Committee, they interpreted this meetness and convenience not in relation to the needs of the public, but in relation to the individuals who were candidates for earning a living in this way. 'I have been perpetually met with objections,'

he said, 'on the score of its being an encroachment upon
the liberties of the subject to refuse a licence to every person
certified as of decent character, and objections in reference to the
principles of free trade, as if the morals and happiness of the
working classes ought to be matter of free traffic for the benefit
especially of persons who, tired of honest industry in their
trades, desire to earn a living by acting as landlords of tippling-
houses.'[11]

Thus it came about that the proportion of licences to population in those days seems quite fantastic to a modern view. In
Edinburgh, in 1829 the number of certificates for licences
granted within the Royalty was 915; in April 1833 the number
was 736; but even this to the population of the Royalty, which
was 55,232, meant a licence to every fifteenth family.[12] Again,
'Glasgow in 1832 contained 19,467 families, with 1,360 spirit
dealers, making one to each 14 families; every fourteenth family
is a spirit dealer in the Royalty. Glasgow and its suburbs, taken
together, contains 40,000 families, with 2,198 spirit dealers,
making one to each 18 families.' The smaller towns were not
noticeably better. Renfrew had one spirit dealer to 18 families,
Greenock one to 19, Port Glasgow one to 15, while Dumbarton,
burgh and parish, with 804 families and 71 spirit dealers, had
one to eleven and a half families. Nor was the position appre-
ciably better in county areas. Taking the Lower Ward of Lanarkshire along with Renfrewshire and Dumbartonshire together,
there was one spirit dealer for every twenty and a half families.[13]
In 1841 in the working-class parish of St. David's, Dundee, with
9,264 inhabitants, there were 11 bakers' shops and 108 publicans; and George Lewis estimated that the licensed places drew
more than a fourth part of the entire earnings of the working
classes.[14] At the same period it was estimated that the quantity of
spirits consumed in Scotland was 23 pints yearly per head of the
population, as compared with 13 pints in Ireland and 7 in
England.[15] Sheriff Alison, referring to Cleland's Statistics of
Glasgow, could assert in 1840 that 'at Glasgow nearly 30,000
persons are every Saturday night in a state of brutal intoxication,
and every twelfth house is devoted to the sale of spirits'.[16] Two
generations earlier, in 1764, Thomas Reid, the philosopher, had
told a friend in Aberdeen that he had not heard any swearing
in the streets nor seen a man drunk since he came to Glasgow.[17]

It is not surprising that Matthew Leishman, minister of Govan, referring to the inns and alehouses of his parish, declared: 'These are so numerous as to form a great moral nuisance. Their pestiferous effects on the health and virtuous habits of the people are only too apparent.'[18] Sheriff Alison, commenting on the criminal statistics, wrote: 'In Scotland it may safely be affirmed that four-fifths, probably seven-eighths, of the crimes which are committed originate in the effects of, or the desire for, whisky.' Alison, like other observers, deplored the reduction of the duty on spirits and the consequent increase in consumption. 'This prodigious increase has done more to demoralize the lower orders than any other measure in the memory of man. It is amply sufficient to account for the great increase in the amount of crime during the same period. . . . In Scotland the number committed for serious offences in 1823 was 1,479: in 1837 it was 3,126. In Glasgow and Edinburgh the number of crimes has been more than quadrupled since the reduction of the duties on ardent spirits.'[19]

By the later 1820's, there were two men in the West of Scotland who not only deplored the situation, but were greatly exercised in conscience over it. One was John Dunlop (1789–1868), who has the best right to be acclaimed as the founder of the temperance movement in Great Britain. Born at Greenock on the second of August 1789 Dunlop entered Glasgow University in the autumn of 1801 and resided in the city with Stevenson Macgill, at that time minister of the Tron parish. After his Arts course he studied law at Glasgow and Edinburgh, settled as a solicitor at Greenock in 1810 and continued there till 1838 when, having succeeded to the lands of Gairbraid through the death of his maternal aunt, he removed to London in order to take general charge of the growing temperance movement. During his professional career in his native town Dunlop became an elder of the Church of Scotland and engaged in many public activities. He was a Justice of the Peace, secretary of the Greenock Infirmary, secretary of the Greenock Chamber of Commerce, a Sunday School teacher and an active supporter of the Savings Bank movement, the Missionary Societies, and the adult education of the artisan classes. He was first led to deplore intemperance by a visit which he paid to the Continent in 1828, when he was impressed by the moral advantage which France enjoyed as compared with Scotland, through the comparative sobriety of her people. About the same time he received some information about temperance societies, with a pledge against ardent spirits, recently founded in the U.S.A., and he approached influential people seeking to introduce such societies into Scotland, but without success.

Greenock seems to have been the Geneva of this new reformation. Not only was it Dunlop's birthplace and, as we shall see, the home of the first general temperance society in Scotland, but as early as 1818 one hears of two societies at Cartsdyke in the east part of Greenock which anticipated the later temperance societies. One was known as the Regular Society and its object was to promote sobriety by using intoxicating liquors, both distilled and fermented, in moderation. The other was called the Moderation Society and took as its basis abstinence from ardent spirits.[20] One hears also of discussions on total abstinence in the Reformed Presbyterian community at Greenock and Paisley, of lectures in the Greenock Institution of Arts and Sciences in 1825–6 and later by Dr. J. B. Kirk, who proved that alcohol was the same in nature whether found in distilled or fermented liquors.[21]

The other man whose conscience, like Dunlop's, was sensitive to the problem was William Collins (1789–1853), founder of the famous publishing house, who became an elder with Chalmers at the Tron and then at St. John's, and was to take a leading part in-promoting Chalmers's plans for church extension in Glasgow.

Dunlop's private conversations with benevolent and influential individuals in Glasgow, Edinburgh, and elsewhere did not afford him much encouragement, but by August 1829 he managed to get twenty gentlemen to meet him in the Religious Institution Rooms in Glasgow, including one minister who had prepared a resolution in advance. Having heard what Dunlop had to say about the extent of the evil and the methods of the American societies, the minister produced his resolution which, while thanking Dunlop for his address, affirmed that no such society would work in Scotland.[22] The resolution failed to find a seconder; and the uneasy silence which followed was dramatically broken by William Collins who rose to his feet and said with considerable emotion that he had had his attention drawn to the painful subject of intemperance in the district of which he had charge as an elder and that his heart had been so burdened by it that often he could not sleep at night. He had pondered and planned without effect, but now for the first time he saw a ray of hope.[23] This impressive statement encouraged others to express similar views, and the upshot was that Dunlop was asked to continue his investigations and report to another meeting in a few weeks. Having prepared his first lecture on 'The Extent and Remedy of National Intemperance', Dunlop came up to Glasgow to deliver it in September 1829. He could find no church or chapel that would be granted him for the purpose; but at length Professor Dick of the Secession Church on the score of old acquaintanceship granted the use of his divinity hall. Very few ministers intimated the lecture to their congregations on the Sunday, but on the Monday evening the lecturer found the hall full, and at the door a group of divinity students jocularly discussing the subject. Dunlop failed, however, at this stage to persuade his Glasgow friends to found a temperance society, and he was driven back upon his native town of Greenock to make a beginning there. As he told the Select Committee in 1834, 'I published my lecture, and instituted the first general Temperance Society in Scotland on the 6th of October 1829, a female one having been a few days previously instituted by a friend, Miss Allan, in the village of Maryhill, near Glasgow.'[24] The two societies flourished so well that they soon proved to interested onlookers that temperance societies with a pledge could succeed in Scotland. Accordingly a society was formed in Glasgow in November 1829, and William Collins was the first name on the list of male members of the Glasgow and West of Scotland Temperance Society.[25] Societies were soon formed in other centres and both Dunlop and Collins found many opportunities as temperance speakers. In June 1830 the first number of a temperance periodical, *The Temperance Record*, was issued, being printed and published by W. Collins, Glasgow.[26]

One aspect of the subject which specially occupied Dunlop's attention was what he was wont to call the 'artificial drinking usages'. 'There has been constituted with us,' he wrote, 'a conventional and artificial connexion between liquor and courtesy and business: and this unnatural conjunction is not, as in some other places, occasional, but nearly universal. . . .'[27] Dunlop was zealous in gathering information about such usages, and an

astonishing number and variety he found. He could tell the
Select Committee in 1834 about sixty-two and he had more still
to investigate.[28] In large works such as cotton-mills, when a man
left one department for another he had to pay a fine in drink.
If a workman's wife had a child, he must pay a fine—for a girl
one bottle of whisky and for a boy two bottles. In the print-
fields the sum of £7 was extorted from every boy admitted as an
apprentice. This was put into a fund which, when it amounted
to £50, was expended in a general debauch, where men, women,
and even children took part and a whole district might be affected
by drunkenness for a fortnight. 'At laying foundations of houses,
fixing joists, delivering keys, at launching ships, at attendance
on Friendly Societies, and almost on every occasion that people
meet to adjust common business: and at such a variety of times
and circumstance as that it is a perfect science to know them all
in every department of affairs, and of domestic life.'[29] A large
number of these customs or usages Dunlop found to be quite
recent, probably not more than of thirty years' standing, and he
reported that people complained sometimes that 'individuals of
dissolute habits in manufactories made a business of inventing
new usages and procuring their establishment'.[30]

Even the ministry had its drinking usages. 'In some presbyteries,' Dunlop told the Select Committee, 'the presbyterial
dinner is furnished with liquor, not by each member present
paying his direct proportionate share, but by fines imposed on
various occasions. When a clergyman gets a new manse he is
fined in a bottle of wine; when he has been newly married, this
circumstance subjects him to the same amicable penalty; the
birth of a child also costs one bottle, and the publication of a
sermon another. And as all ministers do not get manses, wives,
and children, or publish sermons, therefore, in order to equalize
matters, bachelors who have not married after a certain interval,
or those who in the marriage state have no family, or who do not
get a new manse, and so forth, are all fated to be put on the list
and fined for omission, as others have been for commission, so
that no man escapes. In short, many trivial circumstances are
made the occasion of amercement for liquor; and a particular
church-officer, unknown in primitive times, called the comp-
troller, is appointed to attend to this business, and so to adjust
the various mulcts as to prevent one member from paying out

of his course. . . .'[31] Dunlop's opinion of the class incidence of drinking uses was as follows: 'If we divide the society of North Britain into six gradations, commencing with the nobility and ending with the labourer and beggar, we shall find that in all these departments, except the highest, the use of wine and spirits, as the instrument of courtesy and compliment, is general; but becomes more and more straitly and imperatively such the lower we descend'.[32] Many masters were accustomed to pay the wages of their workmen in a public house: and many, to save the trouble of procuring change, gave pound notes among a number of workmen, who thereupon adjourned to the public house in order to change them. The public houses, accordingly, were well furnished on Saturday nights with change and drink, and the ordinary rule was that sixpence must be drunk for every pound changed. Needless to add, sometimes besides the sixpence the greater part of the wages went in drink. Moreover, the great occasions of family life had their drinking usages. 'Besides the profuse drinking that occurs on the immediate occasion of a birth or funeral, the general practice throughout the country among the lower classes is to give a glass to everyone that comes into a house after a birth till the baptism. This is sometimes the sole reason for precipitating the rite, sober people wishing to dismiss the whisky-jar as soon as possible. On the event of a decease, everyone gets a glass who comes within the door until the funeral and for six weeks after it.'[33]

Dunlop saw clearly that the formation of temperance societies would be in vain unless the usages could be broken, and he realized also that it did not require all the inhabitants of a district or all the members of a group or trade to be convinced on the point, but that 'a very few determined persons, by combining together, will demolish a usage'.[34] He recommended therefore to the societies a double procedure, 'first, a general combination of as many as can be obtained in any district against all the usages; and second, specific dealing with an individual usage in a particular class, profession, manufactory, or workshop.'[35]

Collins was able to serve the cause not only by lecturing and instituting societies, but by generous contributions and by the use of his printing press. By the summer and autumn of 1830 he was addressing meetings in some of the large towns of England and in November of that year he was founding London's first temperance society.[36] Meantime the cause prospered in Scotland, and by the end of 1830 about one hundred temperance societies, based on the principle of abstinence from spirits, had sprung up in different parts of the country with a membership of some 15,000 persons.[37] Before long, however, differences began to appear. John Dunlop had held from the beginning that the desirable course was abstinence from all intoxicating drinks, but finding many who objected to united action in any form and knowing that ale and porter were now little used in Scotland, especially by the working classes, he did not insist on their being included. The pledge of the Greenock society banned wines and spirits, but said nothing of other drinks, though a small group of eleven members had taken a total abstinence pledge and had their names in the register marked by a cross in red ink.[38] None of the early societies were total abstinence societies. They interpreted temperance as abstinence from spirits alone or from wines and spirits. Some of their members, however, began to hold that wine and beer should also be banned. Dunlop reports that in September 1830 a total abstinence society was constituted at Dunfermline, and two others, at Paisley and at Tradeston, Glasgow, were formed in January 1832.[39] When John Dunlop came out on the total abstinence side he was disappointed to find how few of his influential associates he could carry with him. 'When however the gentry and high ecclesiastical and official parties, who had joined the original movement against ardent spirits, found that it was now expected they should themselves make a sacrifice, and abandon their own potations, they forsook their colours and retired out of opposition to the rampant national enemy. . . . It was well there were a few among the middle ranks remained to struggle; and that the Peasantry and Commonalty (to some extent at least) were sounder at heart.'[40]

Edward Morris, who became a champion of the teetotal cause, reported a belief that 'the first pledge was a kind of artful combination of the upper classes against the toiling portion of the community by "keeping back whisky from the common people, and retaining the malt liquor, the wine, cyder and perry for ladies and gentlemen". This idea, though a delusion, greatly kept back the working people from 1829 to 1836 from joining the old temperance ranks.'[41] In September 1836, under the leadership of Morris, a Glasgow Radical Temperance Society with a teetotal pledge was formed. The 37 members, if one may judge from their descriptions and addresses, were mostly of artisan rank.[42] Twelve days later an Edinburgh Total Abstinence Society was formed,[43] and about the same time a total abstinence society was begun at Greenock under Dunlop's leadership.[44] From that time the old temperance, or moderation societies, seem to have died out, giving place to those with a total abstinence pledge.

William Collins was one of those who believed in the abolition of spirit drinking, but he was not prepared to advocate a total abstinence which would forbid the use of light wines. In the summer of 1834 he, along with John Dunlop and Sheriff Campbell of Paisley, was presenting facts and figures before a Select Committee of the House of Commons 'appointed to inquire into the extent, causes and consequences of the prevailing vice of intoxication among the labouring classes of the United Kingdom'. Shortly after his old temperance society in Glasgow was wound up in favour of an absolute 'long pledge' society which he felt he could not support, and he was left with a debt of £200 to meet.[45] In 1837 Dunlop wrote—'strove with William Collins to go into the new total abstinence plans, in vain.'[46] Again, in March 1838 he recorded, 'Had a conversation, once more, with Mr. William Collins, urging him to teetotalism: on the ground that it would benefit the cause positively, that the original Apostle of Temperance Association in England should take part in the advancing movement. That negatively, his not joining has a bad effect.' Later Dunlop wrote, 'I think I am grateful to him for being the first to encourage me in 1829, and for his gigantic subsequent exertions. I asked him to give me a memoir of his personal operations: this he declined. (At a future period of his life Mr. Collins became a total abstainer, but did not take any active part in the Movement.)'[47]

By 1838 Dunlop was engaged with delegates from societies in numerous places with a view to forming a Total Abstinence Union for Scotland. Among these he mentions one McNair, 'a Glasgow lath splitter, who had himself taught Hebrew to study the Scripture wine question. A Gourock rope spinner did so also.'[48] The Union was formed in the autumn of that year, and then next year divided into two Unions, an Eastern and a Western,[49] and in November 1840 it was reported that 110 societies had joined the Western Union and that accessions to membership were at the rate of 1,500 a month.[50] A notable occasion in Glasgow was Saturday, 17 July 1841, the Fair Saturday, when there was a grand procession of the teetotal societies of the city and neighbourhood, both Roman Catholic and Protestant. The former mustered on the south side of Glasgow Green and the latter on the north side, and they then went in procession through the streets with bands and flags, the local Rechabites leading. Among the speakers was the Rev. Patrick Brewster of Paisley, no stranger to open-air controversy, who was among the Scottish ministers who helped to make the visit to Scotland of the Irish Temperance advocate, Father Matthew, such a success that 40,000 persons are said to have taken the pledge from his hand.[51] In 1844 the Scottish Temperance League came into existence at Falkirk, having for its aim the 'entire abolition of the drinking system', with a personal pledge never to give or take intoxicants. The League had a humble beginning, but, the old Union having been dissolved in 1846, it soon rallied to itself all the most advanced sentiment on the subject, and it is interesting to note that it was Sir William Collins (1817–95), son of the pioneer, who in 1893 laid the Memorial Stone of the Jubilee Buildings of the League.[52]

In his campaign against the drinking usages Dunlop left no stone unturned. He approached leaders of Sunday Schools, Church Extension societies, Savings Banks and Mechanics' Institutes, and could report that he had met with an encouraging response in his attempt 'to get all the institutions of the country set in array against intemperance, because intemperance is set in array against all the useful institutions of the land.'[53] In June 1840 we find him having long conversations with a number of Chartists at Greenock and elsewhere, and the following year he reported, 'We are striving to arouse indignation at the tyranny of the "usages". We twit the Chartists about submitting to these.'[54] Dunlop believed that there had been an enormous increase in drunkenness among the masses in the fifty or sixty years subsequent to 1790. He reckoned that at that time there were perhaps 30 or 40 artificial drinking usages or drink laws and etiquettes: whereas sixty years later they numbered between four and five hundred. He held, too, that ministers and clergy were greatly to blame in that they took little notice of the increase in drunkenness and, neglecting the drinking usages altogether, made no practical movement for reform. In this connexion he remarks that he was fifty years of age before he heard a sermon on national intemperance. On the whole Dunlop had a poor opinion of the social concern of ministers. 'They study,' he remarked, 'Witsius and Mosheim (which is right) but as to present States of Society or our principal social dangers, some reflective coal porters know more than they.'[55] By 1859, however, he can report that in Scotland 800 ministers of the Gospel are said to be 'pledged', besides many divinity and medical students.[56]

Some excuse for the slowness of ministers individually and for the Churches officially to turn their attention to the subject may be found in the fact that they were distracted in the fifteen years following the formation of the first temperance societies, first by the Voluntary controversy and then by the Non-Intrusion controversy. Thus it was not till a few years after the Disruption that there were signs that the Churches had at last awakened to the seriousness of the problem and were aware of their duty to take action. Then within the space of two years each of the principal Presbyterian Churches took a decided step forward. In 1845 a Ministers' Abstinence Society was formed in the United Secession Church, and in 1847, on the union of that Church with the Relief Church to form the United Presbyterian Church, a Total Abstinence Society was instituted, but that Church had no separate Temperance Committee till 1866. In 1847 the Free Church Assembly appointed a Temperance Committee and two years later a Free Church Temperance Society was formed. Its committee included Dr. Thomas Guthrie of Free St. John's, Edinburgh, and the Rev. William Arnot of Free St. Peter's, Glasgow, who had already incurred some unpopularity from his open opposition to the practice of drinking toasts on the occasion of the induction or ordination of ministers.[57] In 1848 the General Assembly of the Church of Scotland appointed a Committee of Inquiry, which gave way to a permanent Committee to suppress intemperance the following year, after it had presented a valuable report. This report, presented to the Assembly of 1849 by the Convener, the Rev. R. H. Muir of Dalmeny, is an epoch-making document. Being based on 478 returns received in response to circulars sent out the previous year, it is the first authoritative statement on the evils of intemperance in Scotland drawn up by any Church. As causes of intemperance mention is made of drinking usages connected with religious services such as baptisms, marriages, and funerals as well as usages associated with certain trades. Other causes mentioned are the multiplication of licences, the opening of public houses on the Lord's Day, the paying of wages on Saturdays and often in public houses, the temptations of feeing markets and the evils of the bothy system. The remedies suggested are in accord with this diagnosis of the disease and include the reduction of licences, the closing of public houses throughout the whole of the Sabbath day, and the discouragement of social habits leading to intemperance. In 1849 also the Free Church Assembly agreed to petition Parliament setting forth the prevalence of intemperance and asking for measures to check the consumption of spirits and to dissociate the sale of spirits from that of groceries. 'This petition,' it has been pointed out, 'is important as marking the beginning of a policy of pressing for legislative action by the state as the responsible body, a policy which did not commend itself to some temperance reformers. . . .'[58]

A pioneer in temperance work among the young was John Hope (1807–93), the Edinburgh lawyer and philanthropist. When over thirty years of age Hope came under serious religious impressions and in November 1839 he became a teetotaller and began to propagate his views with the same zeal, method, and generosity which he later directed to anti-Popery propaganda. A member of St. Andrew's Church, Edinburgh, he remained in the Church of Scotland at the Disruption; and in 1845 he printed and circulated a letter to the General Assembly calling attention to the 'prominent and all-prevailing sin of drunkenness'. In 1847 he prepared a petition to the Assembly, but it was dismissed on the ground that the matter should be brought up through the inferior courts of the Church. In 1848 his petition came to the Assembly again, but as the subject was brought up also by overture from a country Presbytery, it was considered, and the Assembly resolved to appoint a Committee with Mr. Muir of Dalmeny as Convener, Hope accepting the post of Secretary. This was the Committee which prepared the valuable report of 1849.

By this time, too, Hope had launched the British League of Juvenile Abstainers, one of the earliest, if not the earliest, organizations with the aim of educating children to the danger of intoxicants. The first step was taken by the Edinburgh Total Abstinence Society when in January 1846 it issued a circular to the Sunday School teachers of the city inviting them to a conference to consider how the subject could best be brought before children. Before the end of the year two or three children's temperance meetings had been started in Edinburgh and on 1 January 1847 the British League of Juvenile Abstainers was instituted on the principle of abstinence from giving or partaking of alcoholic liquors, tobacco, and opium. (The Band of Hope movement which soon came to be more widespread than the League was begun at Leeds in the autumn of the same year.) The number of the League's meetings increased quickly, but subscriptions for its support did not come in freely. After a time John Hope resolved to take the burden of expenditure on his own shoulders, and he claimed, quite naturally, that the movement should continue in accord with his views. The number of meetings varied from time to time, but eventually it became stabilized at about twenty, and these were carried on at Hope's expense for nearly fifty years.[59] Another venture of his was the British League evening schools, where at his expense free education in ordinary subjects, including book-keeping, drawing, music, and sewing was provided. It was required that no one attending should have the smell of liquor or tobacco upon them, that one night in the week should be reserved for the teaching of abstinence and that a monthly prayer meeting should be observed. These schools continued for a quarter of a century, down to 1874. In 1850 there were seventeen of them, but for most of the time there were five to seven for young men and two for young women.

Hope touched social matters at many other points. In 1846 we find him encouraging a demonstration in favour of Lord Ashley's Ten Hours Bill and inspiring the founding of the Grassmarket Mission which he largely financed. He gave assistance to the movement for obtaining a Saturday half-holiday for workmen and he proved himself an ally of James Begg in the provision of houses for the working classes. He had many other interests, including the 3rd Edinburgh Rifle Volunteer Corps, which he began, and he spent both energy and money with great generosity, making it his rule to support sparingly, or not at all, causes which enjoyed general popularity, and to support to the utmost of his powers causes that others were not likely to favour. It was on this principle that he acted when he neglected many of his interests and left his ample means for the founding of the Hope Trust, directing that a certain amount of the Trust's funds should go to the promotion of total abstinence, including the use of unfermented wine at the Lord's Supper, and that the bulk of the money should be applied to opposition to the spread of Romanism.[60]

To return, however, to the progress of the movement in general, one must note the formation in Edinburgh in 1850 of the Scottish Association for the Suppression of Drunkenness, an influential body of whose members only a few were themselves abstainers—perhaps the first united action since the Disruption of Scottish churchmen of varied opinions for the general good of the land. It was as much a product of sabbatarian as of temperance sentiment. The great increase in spirit drinking in the previous half-century had affected many aspects of life, not least Sabbath observance. That aspect was touched upon by the Act of 1828 for the better regulation of public houses, commonly known as the Home Drummond Act, which may be regarded as almost the first unmistakable sign of public disquiet over intemperance in Scotland. Among other items the Act provided that licences should be granted on condition that the holders did not sell during the hours of divine service. This was taken, however, as giving permission for public houses to open on Sundays except during those hours, and the law courts confirmed that interpretation. The odd result was that, while the Act had not been intended to diminish the powers of the magistrates, the construction put upon it by the courts did in fact curtail their powers and prevented them from shutting the public houses except during the hours of worship. The outcome was deplorable both from the temperance and the sabbatarian point of view. As William Collins told the Select Committee, 'it is the concurrence of time and money, by the payment of the wages on Saturday, that produces the enormous drunkenness on the Sabbath.'[61]

In general there was no definite hour of closing observed throughout Scotland. In Glasgow there were certain local regulations, based on the Home Drummond Act, which provided that public houses should not be open at unseasonable hours, and that was construed to mean after midnight. Similarly in 1848

Edinburgh got a local Act imposing penalties on publicans who sold after eleven o'clock at night.[62] A further step was taken in Edinburgh by Duncan McLaren who was Lord Provost from 1851 to 1854. He called a meeting of the magistrates and prevailed on them to pass resolutions to the effect that, where publicans were charged with offences in contravention of their licences, keeping open their houses on Sunday should be regarded as an aggravation of the offence. As a result fewer public houses kept open on Sundays, and drunkenness perceptibly decreased. This experiment enabled the Lord Provost to have the proposals framed which later received the sanction of Parliament; and it may be claimed that, while the Act was sponsored by Mr. Forbes Mackenzie, M.P. for Liverpool and previously M.P. for Peebles, and is generally known by his name, the real author of it was Duncan McLaren.[63] Apart from his influence, however, opinion had been moving for some time in the direction of the Act's provisions. In 1834 William Collins had proposed to the Select Committee that public houses should be shut down entirely on the Sabbath, [64] and in 1849 the Church of Scotland report had made the same suggestion. That there was need for reform may be judged from the fact that on one Sunday in 1853 it was found that 312 out of 975 licensed houses in Edinburgh were open, and out of a population of 155,680 there entered these houses 22,202 men, 11,981 women, 4,631 children under 14 and 3,032 children under 8—a total of over 41,000 persons. On the evening of Sunday, 29 October 1848 it was found that 1,097 public houses were open in Glasgow. [65]

The Forbes Mackenzie Act, which came into force in June 1854, may justly be regarded as the most important landmark in the history of temperance legislation in Scotland. Its leading provisions were: the abolition of the system of selling liquor in grocers' shops for consumption on the premises; the closing of all public houses, not specially licensed as hotels, between the hours of eleven in the evening and eight in the morning: and the abolition of the sale of liquor throughout the entire Sunday, except in hotels, and there only to lodgers and *bona fide* travellers. The success of the Act was notable. Duncan McLaren got parliamentary returns on the subject and on analysing them in 1858 came to the conclusion that 'the number of cases of drunkenness alone and drunkenness combined with crime was 165 per cent.

greater on Sundays under the old law than under the new in the chief towns of Scotland, including a population exceeding a million'.[66]

Of the four main methods of dealing with the problem of intemperance—legislative, reformative, educative, and counter-attractive—we have seen that the legislative achieved an important success in the Forbes Mackenzie Act. The reformative is not susceptible of precise assessment, but there is good reason to believe that within the period under review it had many individual successes to its credit, for at that time the crusade against drink partook of the nature of religious revivalism, evoking devoted leadership and mass enthusiasm far beyond the ordinary scope of philanthropic activity. The educative aspect, inseparable from the others, can be traced throughout; it was particularly apparent in the efforts which John Hope directed towards children and young people and in the dissemination of cheap and popular literature. The counter-attractive method also was not overlooked by the zealous pioneers of the early period. John Dunlop, for instance, complained to the Select Committee in 1834 that, while in most of the old burghs of Scotland ground had been set aside for the health and recreation of the people, scanty provision was made in the newer towns and villages that had arisen. He declared his conviction that the people, and especially the young, ought to have ground appropriated for recreational purposes. 'I do not think,' he added, 'that mere literary and scientific education will generate that change of heart required in Scripture or advance morality to a sublime and Scriptural pitch, but it will tend, I think, to reform grosser habits, and drunkenness in particular', and he assured the Committee, on the basis of his own teaching experience, that 'the operatives' could be taught such cultural subjects as political economy, the theory of government, and general history.[67]

Sheriff Campbell also told the Committee that a taste for exercise and amusement in the open air might tend to weaken the existing propensity to resort to tippling-houses as the most frequent mode of relaxation and enjoyment, and regretted that facilities available to the manufacturing population were so few.[68] Edward Morris likewise records the beginning of temperance coffee houses and hotels on the teetotal plan and mentions that he and others of his Radical Temperance Society in Glasgow took a strong interest in combating what he calls 'shop-slavery', that is, long hours in shops, warehouses, cotton-mills, and other establishments.[69] Perhaps just as important was an institution coeval with the temperance societies—the temperance soirée. The first seems to have been held under the auspices of the Tradeston, Glasgow, Temperance Society; and the idea spread and speedily established itself as a demonstration that a social gathering did not need intoxicants to promote good fellowship.[70]

Dr. J. R. Fleming, noticing that William Collins and another Glasgow pioneer, Robert Kettle, had held office under Chalmers, declared that we are bound to trace to him more than to any other the moral enthusiasm that from the first inspired the Scottish Temperance Movement. Though he never became a pledged abstainer he was among the first to be convinced of the necessity of an active campaign against the drink curse that had descended upon his country, and in the last year of his life he made the characteristic remark: 'The temperance cause I regard with the most benignant complacency; and those who stand up in their pulpits and denounce it I regard as a set of theological greybeards.'[71]

PATRICK BREWSTER
AND SCOTTISH CHARTISM

CHARTISM may be said to have arisen from a combination of three factors. There was disappointment with the failure of the Reform Act of 1832 to give any political status to the masses from whose zealous agitation the Reform movement had largely derived its success. There was a swing-back to the method of political agitation after the triumph of the masters in the early thirties, symbolized by the collapse of Owen's Grand National Trade Union and the transportation of the Tolpuddle Martyrs. There was also the economic pressure of the slump period after 1836, especially in the north of England. The roots of Chartism were thus partly political and partly economic, and the outcome was the drafting of the People's Charter in the spring of 1838. It made six demands—manhood suffrage, vote by ballot, annual Parliaments, abolition of the property qualification for members of Parliament, payment of members of Parliament, and equal electoral districts. All but one of these demands—that for annual Parliaments, which was doubtless the most radical of them all—have since been granted, without any dramatic or profound social consequences, which would seem to confirm the view that political reform is much less effective in producing social change than the Chartists and their opponents alike believed.

Associations were formed throughout the country to advocate the six demands and the Charter thus became the rallying point of a movement which lasted for more than ten years, flaring up at times into violent agitation, but suffering a rather inglorious defeat in 1848, and slowly dying thereafter. These demands, extremely radical at the time, seem harmless enough now, and it is difficult to realize that to be a Chartist during the decade 1838–48 produced something of the same shock to upper and middle-class mentality that being a Communist does today. Part of the reason no doubt was that memories of the excesses of the French Revolution were still potent; but much of the fear of Chartism must also be attributed to the fact that some Chartist leaders used language which seemed to prove that their objectives went far beyond the six demands and that their methods might involve confiscation, violence, and bloodshed.

Like all radical movements Chartism attracted a number of cranks and fanatics. Moreover, since those who are unorthodox enough in politics to take up an unpopular radical point of view are frequently also unorthodox in religion, there were to be found Chartist working men who professed a type of rationalism nourished on the writings of Tom Paine. Hence while Chartism alienated some who sympathized with the Charter by the violence of its invective and others by its presumed designs on property, it alienated perhaps a greater number by its supposed hostility to religion and the family. In fact the great mass of Chartists had no hostility to religion, the family or the rights of property, and no intention of breaking out into revolutionary violence. They did not know what they would do with the vote once they had got it: all they knew was that they wanted to curb oppression, improve their conditions of life, and make society more just and happy. The first step seemed to be to win the vote and then to send men to Parliament who would really represent them. All this, which might conceivably have remained a mere opinion, became a compelling force in the hearts of many, partly through unemployment and poverty, and partly through the new English poor-law of 1834, which did indeed reduce the old chaos to a more rational and uniform system, but at the cost of arousing the resentment of the working classes against the harshness of the workhouse test and the tyranny of petty officials.

A recent study of Scottish Chartism[1] has shown that in several important respects Chartism in Scotland must be regarded as almost an independent movement. The sharp reaction which England witnessed against the new poor-law was lacking in Scotland. The poor in Scotland had always been accustomed to look to the charity of friends and neighbours as well as to the parish authorities for help, and the pitifully meagre allowances which they were awarded were so much a matter of use and wont as to cause no excessive resentment at this period. Further, though there were industrial depressions in Scotland in 1839,

1842, and 1848 they were less serious than in England. Certain groups of workers in Scotland experienced very hard times—coal-miners, for instance, and still more the hand-loom weavers—but, on the other hand, there were trades that were flourishing due to the construction of railways and the production of pig-iron and machinery. On the whole the period was one of economic progress for Scotland.

Another factor in the situation, of little weight in England but of importance in Scotland, was the Irish immigrant. Many of these were miners and hand-loom weavers, both poorly-paid trades, yet the support they gave to Chartism in its early and most significant stages was slight. Two reasons have been suggested: that their conditions in Scotland, though bad, were superior to what they had left in Ireland; and that being un-educated immigrants they took some time to emerge from their ignorance and apathy about political matters in their adopted country.

Though the physical-force Chartists had some support in Scotland, the movement was mainly in the hands of men who believed in moral force, in the importance of education, and in the possibility of middle-class co-operation. They brought, moreover, a semi-religious approach which issued in a most distinctive development, the rise of Christian Chartist Churches. One of the Chartist papers declared in March 1840 that 'in every district there ought to be a Chartist Church planted for the benefit of Chartist families', and it recognized that to attract the people more than preaching would have to be offered. 'It is also necessary that baptism and marriage should be regularly dispensed by Chartist missionaries, and likewise the ordinance of the Lord's Supper, otherwise the parish and voluntary clergymen will keep a tenacious hold of Chartist families.'[2] In May the *Circular* published the 'first Chartist sermon preached in Scotland', the text being, 'Beware of false prophets, . . . by their fruits shall ye know them'.[3] Quite a number of Chartist Churches were founded in cities and towns throughout the country, and several had schools attached to them. Behind this development lay the conviction that the Established Church, and indeed the other Churches, too, were hostile to Chartism and generally uninterested in educational, social, and political progress. Chartists also felt impelled to repudiate the charges of 'infidelity' levelled

at them, and to show that Biblical religion included denunciation of oppression and the call to labour for the welfare of one's
fellows. The tone of these Churches depended on the local
leaders. All the Churches were politico-religious bodies in the
sense that they all supported the Charter, but, says Dr. Wright,
they 'never gave real cause to suspect that they behaved otherwise than as truly religious bodies'.⁴ All declared their opposition
to war, not on purely pacifist grounds but because wars were
waged in the interests of others than the working-class. Temperance propaganda was a strong feature of many Chartist
Churches. Their supporters were ordinary working-class folk
with a long religious tradition in their blood, who were hungry
for a message readily applicable to their immediate situation.
Dr. Wright sums up their career thus: 'Had the Established
Church moved in response to the Industrial Revolution there
would have been no Chartist Churches. When Chartism—and
its Churches—died, many were re-absorbed into the new Free
Church or some of the smaller independent sects. A minority
left organized religion entirely, lured away by scientific socialism.
The Chartist Churches officially were a complete failure—but
they helped the Scottish working class to develop valuable
powers of independent thought and organization.'⁵

If any town in Scotland could be regarded as specially miserable during the Chartist era, that town was Paisley, for the decay
of the shawl industry which occupied so large a place in the
town's economy left it 'the most chronically depressed of Lowland industrial centres. Between 1841 and 1843, 67 out of 112
manufacturing firms in the locality failed, with losses totalling
three-quarters of a million. Parochial relief to the unemployed
had to be permitted, in violation of the law, and employment was
afforded by the provision of looms and of allotments, while some
£50,000 was subscribed in charity.'⁶ Distress became so serious
that the Government sent a commissioner to investigate, and he
reported that the workers in Paisley were largely employed in
the shawl manufacture, that in January 1842, 12,703 persons out
of a population of 48,416 depended for subsistence on what they
could get from relief funds, and that in many houses there was
no furniture at all.⁷ It is not surprising that Paisley should have
become a strong centre of Chartism, but to the men of that day
it was more surprising that the most prominent local leader,

indeed one of the leaders of the Scottish Movement generally, should be a minister of the Church of Scotland, one of the two ministers of Paisley Abbey.

A native of Jedburgh and a younger son of a distinguished family which included Sir David Brewster the scientist, Patrick Brewster at the age of thirty was inducted to the second charge of Paisley Abbey in 1818. The first period of his ministry may be dated from that year till 1835, seventeen years during which he seems to have kept clear of controversy, devoting himself to his studies and parochial affairs but taking no open part in political matters. Less than eighteen months, however, after Brewster came to Paisley there were extraordinary scenes witnessed in the town which may have had considerable influence on the young minister's views of public policy. On Saturday 11 September 1819 there was a great Radical gathering at Meikleriggs Muir. Contingents, marching in military fashion and carrying banners with political slogans, assembled from many towns and villages in the west of Scotland. The gathering was an indignation and mourning meeting on account of the 'Peterloo Massacre', when at Manchester cavalry charged the mob, killing eleven persons and wounding some four hundred, including over a hundred women. The Paisley gathering was dispersing in orderly fashion when the ill-advised zeal of a special constable caused an uproar which speedily developed into fierce rioting that soon spread through the town. Cavalry were sent for and arrived from Glasgow on Sunday morning: some infantry followed on Monday; but it was not till Friday that the town was sufficiently quiet for the troops and special constables to be dismissed. The state of affairs during the intervening days may be gathered from the fact that Paisley had the Riot Act read to its citizens on four out of five successive days. One result was that the magistrates made representations that they could not keep the unruly portion of the inhabitants in order unless they had some military force at hand. The Government accepted that plea; barracks were built, and Paisley became and remained for about a century a garrison town.[8] The soldiers from the barracks figure in Patrick Brewster's career, as we shall see. As for the rioting, one need not suppose that it alone produced his 'moral force' views. Christian principle and political wisdom would lead him to the same conclusion; but what he saw in 1819 may well have confirmed

his opinion that there was no hope of social and political relief
to the poor through violence.

In 1832 Paisley like many other centres in Scotland had a
serious outbreak of cholera, and not the only one in the first
half of the century. An average of thirty fresh cases occurred
weekly for several months, and out of a total of 769 victims there
were 446 deaths. It was a time of severe strain for the doctors
and ministers of the town; but it evoked much charitable effort
and led to some cleansing of foul places. A Board of Health was
formed, of which the ministers were members. A special hospital
for cholera patients was established, regulations were drawn up
for the guidance of the public and the streets were fumigated,
the house windows being open to admit the fumes of disinfec-
tants.[9] One may be sure that the lessons of this trying experience
were not lost on Patrick Brewster. Epidemics might produce
special efforts, sanitary measures might remedy obvious conditions of filth; but poverty, overcrowding, and unemployment
remained, leading to dull despair or menacing unrest. One may
reasonably assume that those terrible months of 1832 completed
Brewster's education as a reformer and crystallized convictions
which had been slowly forming in his mind to take his stand
publicly on the side of the poor and the oppressed.

The new epoch in Brewster's career may be dated from 22
September 1835 when he attended a public dinner given in
Glasgow to Daniel O'Connell, and next day drove out with
O'Connell to Paisley where he was present at a public meeting
in honour of the Irish leader. On 4 November Paisley Presbytery
resolved by a large majority 'to record their marked disappro-
bation of Mr. Brewster's conduct in attending the public dinner
given to Mr. O'Connell in Glasgow on the 22nd of September
last, as unseemly and disrespectful to the principles of the
Church of Scotland'.[10] This rebuke was not left unanswered, for
on 12 May 1836 Brewster's friends held a meeting in the
Abbey Church to vote him an address expressive of the respect
and esteem in which he was held. This was probably done in
view of the fact that the Synod of Glasgow and Ayr the previous
month had approved of the action of the Presbytery of Paisley in
taking Brewster's conduct into its consideration, but had dis-
approved of making his conduct the subject of public discussion,
and had remitted to the Presbytery 'to converse with him in

private and to admonish him to be more on his guard against giving offence in future'. Brewster had appealed against this judgment to the General Assembly; but when his appeal was taken up by the Commission of Assembly on 2 June it was dismissed and the sentence of the Synod affirmed. A few days later the Presbytery appointed a Committee to converse with Brewster in private, and on 6 July 1836 it is recorded that he 'expressed regret that he had given offence to the Presbytery and to the Church in the matter referred to', whereupon the Moderator suitably admonished him.[11]

These, however, were merely preliminary skirmishes compared to the battles still to come. Brewster was an avowed Chartist, but he was a leader of the 'moral force' wing of the movement and was firmly opposed to any suggestion of violent methods in prosecuting the claims of the Charter. In 1839 he appeared in a public open-air debate at Paisley with Feargus O'Connor, a clever but irresponsible leader of the militant section, the point at issue being 'the best method of conducting the movement for obtaining the Charter'. Temporary hustings were erected for the occasion, and each side claimed to have a two-thirds majority over the other.[12] This was bad enough, but from the ecclesiastical point of view worse was to follow.

When the Presbytery of Glasgow met in May 1841 a minister produced a placard announcing that the Rev. Patrick Brewster was to preach on Sabbath 18 April in the afternoon and evening in the Christian Chartist Church, Great Hamilton Street. Such conduct, the minister declared, was 'highly disorderly as giving countenance to a body of men whose principles are unchristian and demoralizing'. A Committee was appointed to inquire into the matter, and it reported a month later that Brewster had preached twice as advertised and that in the opinion of witnesses examined by the Committee, 'the drift and tendency of both discourses was to excite the feelings of the humbler against the higher classes of society.' The Committee were 'unanimously of opinion that such conduct is highly censurable in any minister of the Gospel, involving a violation of ecclesiastical order, a contempt of decency, a profanation of the Lord's Day, a desecration of the Christian ministry as appointed by God to evangelize the poor and a mischievous encouragement of a system of disorganization and misrule both in the Church and in the

State'. It was agreed to report the matter to the Presbytery of Paisley, Brewster's immediate ecclesiastical superior. That court seems to have been in some doubt both as to the regularity of the proceedings of the Presbytery of Glasgow and its own powers in the matter, for there ensued some remitting of the case back and forward between the Presbytery of Paisley and the Synod of Glasgow and Ayr, with Brewster protesting and appealing at every stage.[13] At the same time the Presbytery of Paisley was faced with another charge against Brewster for on 29 January 1842 a paragraph appeared in a Paisley newspaper stating that the commanding officer of the 79th regiment, stationed in Paisley, had withdrawn his men from the Abbey Church on the days when Mr. Brewster preached, because of certain insulting references to the military, and that arrangements had been made with Mr. Brewster's colleague in the charge, Mr. Macnair, to conduct a service for the soldiers in a school-room when Mr. Brewster occupied the Abbey pulpit. Paisley Presbytery thereupon appointed a Committee to meet the commanding officer and obtain details, and that Committee got additional powers later to extend its inquiries into Mr. Brewster's ministrations in general. The Committee learned from Major Riach of the 79th that on 9 January he heard Mr. Brewster preach from the words, 'Thy will be done'. The sermon appeared to him to be of a very inflammatory character, especially considering the state of the manufacturing population of the town at the time. The conduct of the officers in withdrawing their troops had been approved at headquarters. The Committee also reported that many people had been compelled to leave Brewster's ministry on account of his introducing violent language and political dissertations into his sermons. He had also not infrequently held the landowners and aristocracy up as murderers of the poor, as a set of heartless bloodthirsty plunderers who had robbed the people of the land— their inalienable heritage—and who ought to be made to deliver it back, having no better title to it than a slave-owner to his slaves. Mr. Brewster was further stated to have disparaged, from the pulpit, some of the schemes of the Church, not only discouraging the congregation from contributing, contrary to the directions of the General Assembly, but representing that the heathen, proselytized to Christianity through the missionary efforts of the Church, were made twofold more the children of hell than before. He had compared those who had taken a lead in recommending sabbath-observance and family worship and such good practices to the hypocritical pharisees of old. His conduct in preaching in a Chartist Church in Glasgow and in attending Chartist and other meetings where violent language was used and where scenes of questionable propriety were enacted, had likewise given offence and been hurtful to his ministerial usefulness. Finally, the Committee reported that while much of Mr. Brewster's time had of late years been spent in attending political meetings he had not been in the habit, during a long incumbency, of visiting his parishioners as a minister or of directing his pastoral efforts to the spiritual edification and consolation of the sick and dying.

The Presbytery of Paisley on hearing these allegations decided to require Mr. Brewster to produce the objectionable sermons by the next meeting: but this he declined to do and intimated an appeal to the General Assembly. The Presbytery again met, but as the culprit still refused to give up his discourses, it was resolved to refer the whole case to the Assembly and to ask for guidance and for authority to proceed in face of any protests on Mr. Brewster's part. Hence it came about that on Wednesday, 1 June 1842 the Commission of Assembly took up two references from the Presbytery of Paisley with regard to Mr. Brewster—the one concerning the withdrawal of the military from his preaching and the other his preaching in a Chartist place of worship. Members of Presbytery appeared, but not Mr. Brewster. Accordingly the Commission 'sustained the reference, enjoined Mr. Brewster to produce to the Presbytery the sermons therein referred to; found that there are grounds for serving Mr. Brewster with a libel; instructed the Presbytery, in the event of a libel not being tendered by other competent parties before the 1st of July next, to serve Mr. Brewster with a libel, suspend Mr. Brewster from the exercise of his ministerial and pastoral functions till next General Assembly, and authorize the Presbytery to meet at Paisley on Friday next . . . to take steps for carrying this judgment into effect'.[14] Next day, however, Thursday 2 June, Mr. Brewster appeared at the bar and, after explaining how he had failed to appear the previous day, he was allowed to address the Commission in his defence. On the Chartist issue, he said that he had been asked by some parties to preach a sermon which he had previously preached in behalf of an emigrant society. He agreed to do so; but asked to have a better lighted Church than the one in which he had preached before. They offered him the Chartist Church and he agreed, subject to the consent of the minister of the parish, which was readily granted. He therefore preached there, as he would have done in the Pope's pulpit or in a theatre, not making himself responsible for the religious opinions of the persons wont to worship there. At the same time he could say for the two men who preached there, that, though one was a carpenter and the other a shoemaker, he would not fear to place either of them side by side with the best minister of the Church of Scotland. As regards the military sermons, he did not wonder at the commanding officer, or men of his class, finding fault with his preaching, but he was ready to defend every word he had said by the Bible, and, in opposition to the officers, he could have the testimony of every soldier in the barracks that they were satisfied with his preaching and held it to be the Gospel. He did not say that all soldiers were human tigers—he said that of the armies of despotic states—but he admitted saying that they were made the instruments of oppression and were little better than slaves. He had also warned his people that no man ought to enlist and sell his moral as well as his physical liberty, and the result had been that, notwithstanding all the distress in Paisley, they had hardly been able to get a single soldier. As for the charge of preaching worldly politics, he said his accusers preached worldly politics as much as he: they preached submission to the civil power, without anyone questioning them; but fault was found with him when he preached justice for the oppressed and bread for the hungry. He denied ever having called the aristocracy heartless murderers of the poor; but he did insist that they had no such absolute unqualified right to their land as to deny a sufficient supply of food for the poor. He was ready to produce his sermons and had always been so, but, since he had appealed from the sentence of the Presbytery on the ground of certain irregularities, he held he would have compromised his appeals had he admitted their jurisdiction. He concluded an address lasting two hours by asking the Commission to dismiss the reference in both cases.[15]

This plea of Brewster's did nothing to induce the Commission to modify its decision of the previous day. Dr. Candlish remarked that Mr. Brewster's speech, instead of shaking his opinion of the previous day's sentence, strongly confirmed it. It was plain that a libel was indispensable for Mr. Brewster's own sake. Mr. Cunningham, later Principal of New College, Edinburgh, agreed with Dr. Candlish that for Mr. Brewster's sake there must be a libel; but he was considerably more sympathetic to Brewster's views. He ventured to say that it might be that in the long run Mr. Brewster might be able to show that there was nothing in his sermons but what was set forth in the strong statements of the Word of God against oppression and tyranny and against tyrants and oppressors, and, if rash language were used in commenting upon them, he must say for himself that he had some sympathy for a man who in the present times brought these strong statements of the Word of God to bear upon society, and he would not be disposed to construe harshly any rash or indiscreet expressions that might be made use of in such discourses. In the meantime, however, the sentence ought not to be altered. So the decision to suspend Brewster and serve him with a libel was re-affirmed.[16]

The case, however, did not follow a plain course, for Brewster set himself to obstruct as far as possible. At the Presbytery of Paisley on Friday 3 June he spoke from two o'clock till eleven o'clock in the evening, and then took nearly two hours the next day to complete his defence.[17] He protested against the demand of the Presbytery for the production of his discourses, maintaining that there had been two references before the Commission and two sets of discourses in question, but that in effect only one of the references had been sustained, and that it could not be clearly ascertained from the sentence of what particular discourses the Commission had required the production. Presumably it was in consequence of such objections plus a refusal to produce any sermons that another reference from Paisley Presbytery in the case of Mr. Brewster came before the Commission on 16 November 1842. This time the Commission 'declined to receive the reference, as not containing any point requiring their interference'. Next day, however, 17 November 1842, the Commission took up a petition from the Presbytery of Paisley and another from the Rev. Patrick Brewster, on the subject of the present state of the poor. Brewster's petition partook of the nature of kite-flying. He recognized that the Evangelical party, dominant in the Church courts, were truly in earnest in urging the spiritual claims of the people, and he had conceived the hope that they might also be led to see the necessity and duty of advocating their civil rights. He accordingly framed a petition in which he pointed out the extreme destitution due to unemployment and, in that connexion, the duty of all Christians and particularly the duty of the office-bearers of the Church as the legal guardians of the poor. His petition then proceeded—'the existing position of the Church on the one hand, and the country and the people on the other, present a most auspicious and providential concurrence of circumstances, of which the Church might wisely and constitutionally avail herself to effect a reconciliation, and even a re-union, with that portion of the people who have been alienated in their affections and separated from her communion, but who are still warmly attached to her principles; and that, strengthened by their grateful and cordial co-operation, the Church might speedily emancipate herself from the state dictation and tyranny, which have so long paralysed her ministrations, cramped her zeal, and destroyed her usefulness; and which, at this moment, threaten her very existence as an Establishment'.[18] Brewster's own account of what happened to his petition is that it 'was courteously received, and then decently interred, by being handed over to one of their Committees'. The official account says: 'The Commission most deeply sympathizing with the sufferings of the working classes and the poor generally, arising from the existing destitution, and looking with anxiety to the prospect of increased distress during the ensuing winter, earnestly urge on all Presbyteries within the bounds of the Church, to use every effort for alleviating that distress, and recommend also to the Committee of the General Assembly on the subject of the Poor, to take this subject into their consideration, and to adopt such steps by communication with the government or otherwise, as they may deem fitted to promote measures calculated to afford the relief so urgently required, and recommending them also to advise with such members of the Church as may have had opportunities of experience in reference to this subject. . . .'[19]

The libel which the Commission had called for was served on 15 February 1843 at the instance of the Marquis of Abercorn, the Earl of Glasgow and other heritors of the Abbey Parish. It extended to 93 pages of manuscript and contained 13 counts—such as the prostitution of the ordinance of preaching by introducing worldly and secular politics and affairs, particularly the Corn Laws, the Poor Laws and the administration thereof, with statements calculated to create hostility between different classes, and bring the Rulers and Government of the country into contempt —with the danger that the working classes, at a time of destitution, might rise in insurrection and cause destruction of property and life. After the libel was served Brewster's friends held a meeting and passed resolutions in his support. A number of the people of the Charleston district also took the opportunity of presenting him with a walking stick with a silver plate bearing a suitable inscription, which, no doubt, was valued by him as some answer to the charge that he had neglected his parochial duties through his involvement in politics.[20]

By the time the General Assembly of 1843 was ready to deal with Mr. Brewster and the libel the Disruption had taken place. Moreover, the decision in the Stewarton case had established the legal point that the General Assembly had no right to do, what after the Chapel Act of 1834 it had done, viz., admit to the Church courts the ministers plus elders of *quoad sacra* parishes. Decisions taken after votes in which such ministers and elders had participated were liable, therefore, to be called in question. It is not surprising, therefore, that when the Assembly on 26 May 1843 came to consider two references from the Synod of Glasgow and Ayr in the case of Mr. Brewster the decision was: 'The General Assembly, in respect of the specialties of this case, agree without a vote to set aside and to cancel the whole proceedings therein, and remit to the Presbytery to receive any new libel which may be tendered, and to proceed with the same according to the rules of the Church.'[21]

Dr. Robert Burns, who had been one of Brewster's chief opponents in Paisley, had left the Church at the Disruption, and presumably the Paisley Presbytery deemed it prudent for the Church to close its depleted ranks in face of the rampant Free Church. At all events the Chartist and Military sermons—though Brewster published them in 1843—seem to have troubled that venerable court no more, for on Wednesday 6 December 1843 it found that 'the libellers have fallen from their purpose, and therefore assoilzie Mr. Brewster'. Brewster's career, however, continued to be attended by controversies until near its end. He died in 1859 and was given a public funeral in Paisley, about 500 people walking in the procession and immense crowds lining the streets. In 1863 a handsome monument was erected over his grave by public subscription.

It appears that for a day or two, if not longer, in the critical year 1843, Brewster hesitated whether or not, like his brothers James and David, to join the Free Church. Writing of the able men at the head of the Free Church, he said, 'There was something so magnanimous, and bearing tokens of such undoubted sincerity in the manly firmness with which they had latterly maintained their position, that my expectations seemed confirmed by their disruption from the Church, and I ventured to think it not impossible that I might yet be permitted to cast my lot with the many zealous men who had followed them out of the Establishment. But the door was quickly barred against me by their illustrious Moderator whose opening speech—cheered to the echo—painfully convinced me that I should have less freedom in the FREE Church, than even within the pale of the Establishment, and that wherever my foot might find a resting place, it could not be among those, who, without one dissentient voice, had solemnly denounced the millions of their oppressed countrymen—to whose liberation I had devoted my humble labours, and who were peacefully and constitutionally seeking the redress of their intolerable wrongs—as anarchists and rebels.'[22] He referred presumably to the paragraph in Dr. Chalmers's opening speech as Moderator of the First Free Church Assembly, in which he stated: 'There can be no common understanding, for there is no common object, between you and the lovers of mischief. The lessons which you inculcate are all on the side of peace and social order. . . . if on the flag of your truly free and constitutional Church you are willing to inscribe that you are no Voluntaries then still more there will be an utter absence of sympathy on your part with the demagogue and agitator of the day—so that in golden characters may be seen and read of all men this other inscription, that you are no anarchists.' A meeting of the Abbey Congregation was held on 5 June 1843 when Brewster moved and an elder seconded a resolution, expressing sympathy with those who had gone out 'in their attempts to obtain for the people the choice of their ministers, and in the noble sacrifices they have recently made in behalf of their non-intrusion principles', but declaring that 'as they have refused to recognize and claim the civil rights of a suffering and oppressed people—rights which it was their peculiar duty as the assertors of the Redeemer's HEADSHIP and the interpreters of his revealed law to vindicate and support . . . this congregation cannot unite or co-operate with them'.[23]

Some extracts from Brewster's sermons may serve to indicate his point of view. 'You cannot separate religion from Politics. The Bible is full of politics; and to imagine that men can be innocent, in giving their support to the measure of unrighteous and oppressive rulers, or in opposing and frustrating those of a just and paternal government, is a thing that will hardly be maintained. . . .'[24] Again, speaking of the Scottish Poor Law he said: 'The system in Scotland is one of fraud and injustice. It sets at defiance all law and right—all humanity and mercy. It has a wisdom of its own, and a worship of its own—the wisdom of the world, and the worship of Mammon. Its constant aim and tendency is to give nothing at all.' Then, turning to sarcasm, he broke out, 'The Patrons of this system believe they have made a discovery, that to deal their bread to the hungry, as God commands them, would be injurious to human happiness and human virtue, and so devotedly self-denying are they, for the good of others—so superhumanly kind to their neighbours,—that rather than hazard the increase of human suffering by feeding the hungry, they will peril their own immortality, by a wilful act of disobedience to God.'[25] Again, he said: 'Those who doubt the EXPEDIENCY of obeying the law in reference to the claims of the industrious poor, must be prepared to have other claims—much less clear in their nature, reason and justice—called in question upon the same ground. . . . If a sufficient portion of the rent of land and of accumulated capital shall be refused to supply the wants of the industrious citizens by whose labour they were produced, it will inevitably come to be made a question, why so large a share of the products of industry should be given to idlers, and why property of any kind should be respected when those who own it are the first to violate the rights of others.'[26] In another sermon he said: 'In the great towns, especially, a large proportion of the Established and Dissenting Churches are mainly occupied by the middle or wealthier ranks of society. These, with their teachers, make an outward and regularly decent profession of Christianity. They make a fair show of the virtues, which, in the estimation of their own class, are necessary to sustain the respectability of that profession, but they are lamentably deficient in the substance and reality of Christian practice.'[27] Following upon that, one is prepared for this declaration: 'There are some admirable exceptions, but generally speaking the great mass of church-goers are UNCHRISTIANIZED. The effect of their cruel injustice to their brethren has wrought a righteous retribution upon their own character, and has sunk them below the level of the human creature. Talk of converting the Heathen to Christianity! Let them first convert themselves.'[28] Some explanation of these bitter words may be found in certain shocking cases of neglect in the Abbey Parish to which reference is made in general terms in the same sermon, but which are more fully set forth in an appendix to the volume of sermons as published. It would appear that the Superintendent and some of the overseers of the poor in the parish were guilty of wanton neglect and cruelty, but that when the Session drew the heritors' attention to the matter, far from censuring or superseding the Superintendent, they actually passed a vote of confidence in him. On this Brewster remarked: 'Cruelly and unjustly as the Scotch parishes have treated their poor, it was reserved for the wealthy heritors of this parish to declare by a PUBLIC ACT that they wished their poor to be starved, and that there was no redress for the most wanton cruelty.'

In the appendix to his published volume of sermons, Brewster took up the charge that the tendency of his discourses was to excite to violence and insurrection, and claimed that he did not advise or encourage any breach of law, pointing out 'that while extensive insurrectionary attacks were made upon property in other parts of Scotland, there was not a single instance of aggressive violence in the town or neighbourhood of Paisley, where the destitution and distress were most prevalent and severe'.[29] Dealing with the question how far he was warranted or required, as a minister of the Church of Scotland, to introduce such topics into his pulpit discourses, he instanced the example of Knox and his successors, and quoted the Scots Confession, Article XV and the First and Second Books of Discipline, also the Act of the Commission of the General Assembly for renewing the Solemn League and Covenant 6 October 1648, which was ratified by an Act of the Committee of the Estates of Parliament 14 October 1648. 'To preach Christ crucified in the sense of the libellers', said Brewster, 'without preaching the UNIVERSALITY of God's law, which Christ *"came to fulfil"* would not be to preach *"the truth as it is in Jesus"*. To preach a mere fraction of revealed truth, without preaching obedience to divine law in all the affairs of life, would neither be preaching the word of God nor the Gospel of Christ. Christ is "PRINCE OF THE KINGS OF THE EARTH", and his *"Kingdom"* though *"not of this world"*, yet *"ruleth over all"*. This is the true HEADSHIP of the Son of God, and not some subordinate matter respecting the election of ministers—the regulation of his worship or the government of his Church. He must be acknowledged and served as the "King of kings, and Lord of lords". We must take the law of his word as our guide and director in all the affairs of life, holding and asserting its SUPREMACY over every other law. . . .'[30]

The Chartist and Military Sermons are certainly clear, vigorous, and forthright; but it is hard to see how they could provide grounds for a libel. It would have been interesting to see how the Presbytery of Paisley, had they proceeded further, would have dealt with such opinions as stand on record in these Sermons, and attempted to show that they were contrary to the Scriptures and the Confession of Faith. Perhaps it was some sense of the difficulty of doing so that made William Cunningham admit that in the long-run Brewster might be able to show that there was nothing in his sermons but what was set forth in the strong statement of the Word of God against oppression and tyranny. Brewster was not content with verbal denunciation. In a letter to the press in May 1841 he claimed that he had 'invited the people of Scotland to form societies . . . and having received assurances of support from various parts of the country, I had organized an association in Paisley, under the name of the Destitute Poors' Protection Society, whose special object is "to obtain immediate and sufficient relief to the poor" '.[31]

It ought to be added that, while Brewster's views were more radical than those of his ministerial colleagues in Paisley, he was not alone in being concerned about the inadequacy of the poor-law. At the meeting of Presbytery which remitted to the Synod the charge of Brewster's having preached in a Chartist Church in Glasgow, Dr. Robert Burns brought forward a report on the condition of the poor in Paisley, and a special meeting for considering it was appointed.[32] Further, both in May 1841 and May 1842 Brewster proposed that the Presbytery overture the General Assembly on the state of the Poor and the Working Classes and on both occasions the overture was unanimously adopted. In the first overture the Assembly was asked 'to petition the Legislature for an inquiry into the state of the poor in general, and of the industrious classes in particular, and to recommend to Kirk-Sessions to use their best endeavours in the meantime to obtain for the destitute immediate and adequate relief'. In the second overture the Assembly was asked 'to encourage and support the Government in the attempt to amend the poor law, if that should be found necessary, or to improve the present system of management and render it more accordant to the spirit and meaning of the poor laws of Scotland'.[33]

Unlike Chalmers and most of his contemporaries Brewster rejected Malthusianism as an 'infidel philosophy' opposed to the 'authority and requirements of revelation'.[34] Moreover he was alive to the social as well as the individual causes of distress, as when he declared that the combined effect of the tax on food and 'the progress of chemical science and mechanical invention has been to throw off a considerable portion of the people as supernumeraries'.[35]

Though a moral-force Chartist Brewster incurred the odium attaching to an inciter to insurrection. On the other hand he aroused the hostility of physical-force leaders like Feargus O'Connor and even experienced a temporary unpopularity with the mob, which led to his being howled down at a demonstration in his own town in 1848.[36] Like some other progressive ministers in Scotland he supported Joseph Sturge's Complete Suffrage Movement and the Anti-Corn Law League; but he saw no reason why middle-class movements like these should be singled out for clerical blessing on moral grounds while more popular agitations were left alone. He declared that what sustained him in the course he had taken was both the deliberate acquiescence of his own mind and the sympathy of his fellow-countrymen, expressed in addresses which were adopted at public meetings in most of the principal towns of Scotland—meetings organized, one supposes, by the local Chartist groups.

Brewster was a strong opponent of slavery and the slave trade, and a strong advocate of Catholic emancipation, though in his later years, after one of his daughters had gone over to the Roman Catholic Church, he appeared bitterly anti-Romanist. He abstained from intoxicating liquors and was for many years an office-bearer of the Paisley Total Abstinence Society. All in all he was decidedly a man in advance of his time, though public opinion advanced so markedly in his direction during his public career that his niece could claim that 'his riper views, indeed, were not more radical than those brought into practice by the Conservative Government of 1866'.[37]

One must acknowledge that Brewster revelled in controversy and asserted his views with undue vehemence at times; but, having regard to the whole trend of his career, one may join in the verdict of his Presbytery—'assoilzie Mr. Brewster'. Indeed one may hail him as a modern representative of a tradition which was strong in the immediate post-Reformation era and has never died out in the Church of Scotland—the tradition which asserted the right of the Christian minister to comment on public affairs and apply the law of God as he learned it from Scripture to the laws of the land and customs in every sphere of the national life.

8

JAMES BEGG AND THE
HOUSING OF THE WORKING CLASSES

ERHAPS the most notable of those upon whom the mantle of Chalmers's social concern fell was James Begg (1808–83), minister of Liberton at the time of the Disruption and later minister of Newington Free Church, whose public career links together the era of the Non-Intrusion controversy and that of the Robertson Smith case. In the last period of his life he was prominent as the leader of the die-hard opposition party in the Free Church, recruited principally from the Highlands—opposed to union with the United Presbyterians, to Higher Criticism, to modifying the Confession of Faith, to hymns and instrumental music—and the notoriety which he gained as champion of these increasingly unpopular views has obscured the fame which is his due as an early and zealous social reformer. If he had been killed in the railway accident in which he was involved in 1865, a few weeks before he became Moderator of the Free Church Assembly, instead of being merely injured, his name would be more highly honoured today.

Begg's biographer, Dr. Thomas Smith, suggests that his social views were formed on the model of those of Stevenson Macgill, his Professor of Theology in his student days in Glasgow.[1] It is clear that Begg never regarded religion as separate from the daily life of men, but as bearing upon all educational, economic, and social relations. In a speech on National Education in the Free Church General Assembly of 1850 he declared, 'Whilst I cordially say that everything pertaining to the mere partisan or politician ought always to be banished from the courts of this Church, the social condition and the physical circumstances of the people are matters with which we have much to do.' He went on to refer to a number of examples in the past history of the Scottish Church, from Buchanan and Knox down to Stevenson Macgill, Duncan of Ruthwell and Chalmers, and declared, 'I see these men, great as ministers of Christ, and at the same time prominent in promoting every object by which the temporal prosperity of the people may be advanced.'[2] Again and again in speech and writing Begg defended this position by referring to the comments of the *Shorter Catechism* on the Decalogue, for example, ' "The sixth commandment requireth all lawful endeavours to preserve our own life and the life of others" and "The eighth commandment requireth the lawful procuring and furthering the wealth and outward estate of ourselves and others" thus placing, in effect, our obligation to promote sanitary and social reform on the strongest foundation on which they can rest viz., the direct commandment of God'.[3]

It was in 1849 that Begg came to the front as leader of a movement in Edinburgh for social reform. In January of that year he brought forward in his Presbytery an overture on the state of the Free Church in the poorer districts of large cities with a view to increasing the number and efficiency of Free Church congregations in such needy districts.[4] He followed this up with a communicated article and then a series of long letters in the Free Church newspaper, *The Witness*, edited by Hugh Miller, in which among other things he described some of the terrible conditions prevailing in Edinburgh and dealt with the need of providing better houses for the working classes. The outcome of this propaganda was a meeting in College Street Church on 10 January 1850 at which Begg was the principal speaker. In his address he alluded to the famous Charter and declared that his charter was more extensive and comprised seven or eight points: a universal system of education, involving an improvement both in quantity and quality; the diminution of drunkenness; better dwellings for the working classes—here he mentioned the efforts of one of those present at the meeting, the Rev. William Mackenzie of North Leith, who had succeeded in getting eight self-contained houses erected, with ground in front and let at moderate rents; the provision of washing-houses and bleaching-greens, and here he referred to the exclusion of the public from open spaces such as the Meadows and West Princes Street Gardens; emancipation from feudalism, including the abolition of the law of entail—if there were free trade in land Scotland would be found not to be over-populated, as was often alleged, because so much was uncultivated; the simplification of the

transference of land; the use of criminals and paupers to cultivate waste land and so to contribute to their own support; and
remedies for the misgovernment of Scotland, owing to its neglect
by the Parliament in London. Scotland had only one public
functionary, the Lord Advocate. There ought to be a Secretary
of State for Scotland with a Council of Scotsmen and possibly
even a Scottish Legislative body, if the peculiar problems of the
country were to be adequately faced. On the motion of Mr.
Makgill Crichton of Rankeillour the meeting appointed a committee to consider forming a National Association for the elevation of the working classes.[5] Hence it came about that on
18 January 1850 there was instituted the Scottish Social Reform
Association, with its declared object the promotion of the
economic well-being of the community. It was recognized that
others were labouring in the same field, hence the Association
resolved to keep certain main ends in view. First, the promotion
of all sanitary measures, particularly the erection of improved
houses for workmen and the securing to all of the free use of
public grounds for the purpose of bleaching and of healthful
recreation. Second, the emancipation of the soil and the opening
up of the undeveloped resources of the country by the abolition
of the law of entail and a simplification of the cumbrous and expensive mode of conveyancing. Third, a reform of the pauper
and criminal systems making paupers and criminals as far as
possible self-sustaining, by enforcing productive employment
in lieu of mere maintenance and that without interfering with
the ordinary labour market.[6]

Begg's basic social concern was for the housing of the working
classes. How fundamental he believed this to be may be gathered
from his own words—'Partial remedies for the admitted evils of
society have, in turn, been loudly applauded and eagerly tried by
benevolent and earnest people, only to prove that, whilst the
grand cure for the woes of society is only to be found in the
gospel of the grace of God, and in that new heart and right spirit
without which man must in any circumstances remain depraved
and miserable, the most important physical remedy for the woes
of man is a comfortable and wholesome dwelling.'[7] His interest
in housing went back to the years of his ministry at Liberton. As
he told the Social Science Association in 1858, he had been
minister of one of the richest parishes in Midlothian, and when

he went there in 1835 'although the average rental was about £5 an acre, there was not a ploughman's house with more than one apartment, and some of them were so frail that he was told by the people that the bedposts were the only props to the roof, and that they were afraid to take down their beds lest the whole concern should tumble about their ears'.[8]

Stimulated by indignation at the appalling conditions prevailing in his rural parish, Begg made about 1840 a personal inspection also of the most degraded districts of Edinburgh and Glasgow.[9] The impressions created may be judged from those recorded by other observers. William Chambers, writing to Edwin Chadwick, admitted that in Edinburgh, 'in spite of vigorous regulations to the contrary, the closes which are inhabited by the poorer classes continue in a most filthy condition both night and day. . . . Independently, however, of the insalubrity from this cause, I feel convinced that there is as great a moral evil. The eyes of the people, old and young, become familiarized with the spectacle of filth, and thus habits of uncleanliness and debased ideas of propriety and decency are ingrafted . . . Society, in the densely peopled closes which I have alluded to, has sunk to something indescribably vile and abject. Human beings are living in a state worse than brutes. They have gravitated to a point of wretchedness from which no effort of the pulpit, the press or the schoolmaster can raise them.'[10] Again, J. C. Symonds, one of the assistant hand-loom weaving commissioners, reported: 'I have seen human degradation in some of its worst phases both in England and abroad, but I can advisedly say, that I did not believe, until I visited the wynds of Glasgow, that so large an amount of filth, crime, misery, and disease existed on one spot in any civilized country.'[11] It is not surprising that Edwin Chadwick could write: 'The most wretched of the stationary population of which I have been able to obtain any account, or that I have ever seen, was that which I saw in company with Dr. Arnott and others in the wynds of Edinburgh and Glasgow', and 'It might admit of dispute, but, on the whole, it appeared to us that both the structural arrangements and the condition of the population in Glasgow was the worst of any we had seen in any part of Great Britain'.[12] Chadwick ascribes this partly to sheer lack of houses. —'From a report on the late census, made to the Lord Provost of Glasgow by Mr. Strang, Chamberlain (19 July 1841) it appears that in the most densely peopled part of the town (Blackfriars parish) the population since 1831 has increased 40 per cent., while the number of inhabited houses has not increased at all.'[13]

As we have seen in the parish of Liberton, bad housing was by no means confined to the cities. Dr. Scott Alison of Tranent reported: 'I have seen horses in two houses in Tranent inhabiting the same apartment with numerous families. One was in Dow's Bounds. Several of the family were ill of typhus fever, and I remember the horse stood at the back of the bed. In this case the stench was dreadful. In addition to the horse there were fowls, and I think the family was not under ten souls. The father died of typhus on this occasion.'[14] The same observer, however, reported that the colliers of Tranent had high wages and remarked that 'filth is more frequently evidence of depravity than of destitution'. He also contrasted the condition of the colliery population with that of the agricultural labourers in the vicinity of Tranent, greatly to the advantage of the latter 'in spite of the defective construction of their cottages'.[15]

Just after the Disruption there appears to have been in certain Edinburgh circles an active interest in the housing of the working classes. Among the pioneers was the Rev. William Mackenzie, minister of North Leith Free Church. He had a special dislike of one-roomed houses because of our Lord's command, 'When thou prayest enter into thy closet and shut the door.' As James Begg, too, often insisted, how could one do that in a one-roomed house? With the help of friends he set a scheme going and, as we have already noted, erected some eight or ten houses of a superior kind. This example awoke a response in a neighbour, the Rev. William Garden Blaikie, who coming from Aberdeenshire in 1844 to be minister of Pilrig Free Church was depressed by the unsatisfactory nature of city housing. With his Kirk-Session he approached the Governors of Heriot's Hospital who owned much of the land at Pilrig as well as a row of miserable cottages, built in defiance of sanitary principles and known as Mushroom Row from the rapidity with which they had been built. Rebuffed with scorn Blaikie took counsel with his brother-in-law, Robert Balfour, an insurance manager, and they gathered a group of influential men, formed the Pilrig Model Dwellings Company and obtained a site on Leith Walk. Their first row of cottages was built in 1849 and the fourth and last in 1862. In all the Company erected sixty-two dwellings at a cost of £7,000. They were let at rents ranging from five guineas to £18, the majority being at £7 to £10. In 1892 when most of the original contributors and all the directors except Blaikie were dead the company was wound up and the property passed into private hands. The company had regularly paid a dividend, limited to five per cent., and it had demonstrated that in those days it was possible to build healthy and comfortable cottages to be let at moderate rents and to produce a moderate return on capital invested.[16]

Begg regarded such efforts, good so far as they went, as totally inadequate. 'To any one intelligently contemplating the vastness of the evil to be dealt with, it was evident from the first that you could no more reconstruct the larger portions of great cities, and provide houses for hundreds of thousands of people, by mere speculation or benevolence, than you could feed or clothe the mass of the people by similar means. The mischief had become so great that, in addition to other difficulties, the most vigorous efforts of the whole people themselves, backed by the energetic action of local magistrates, and even of the general Government in the way of removing obstacles, could alone be expected to grapple successfully with a problem so vast and yet so momentous.'[17]

At the request of the Scottish Social Reform Association Begg delivered in his own church on 6 March 1851 a lecture which was published under the title *How every man may become his own landlord*. In this lecture he gave some account of the rise of Property Investment Companies and showed the services they were rendering to some working men. It appeared, however, that increased facilities for purchase while the supply was nearly stationary only drove up prices. It was necessary to increase the supply and to provide better houses. The whole of the outskirts of Edinburgh should be studded with new houses for the working classes, each, if practicable, with a garden. Then it would be possible to buy those in the centre of the city cheaply. 'You will never get the unclean heart of Edinburgh gutted out until you plant it all round with new houses.'[18]

Begg was much impressed by the example of the working men of Birmingham who by joint action had bought up land and built comfortable cottages, thus becoming owners of their own dwellings through money chiefly saved from the public house.

Twice between 1855 and 1858 he brought James Taylor from Birmingham and organized tours with him to some twenty-six of the largest cities and towns of Scotland where at public meetings he explained what could be done. In this movement Begg had the support of Duncan McLaren, later M.P. for Edinburgh, also William Chambers, later Lord Provost, who visited Birmingham and other English cities to see what had been achieved. He gave a lecture in January 1862 which was published as a pamphlet under the title *Building Societies*.[19]

One particular aspect of housing about which Begg was fearlessly outspoken in season and out of season was the bothy system for farm servants. His views may be gathered from a public letter which included this: 'What is a bothy? It is a kind of human stable or cow-house, invented for cheapness by the greedy lairds of Aberdeen and Angus, into which the farm labourers, made in the image of God, are huddled after their work. . . . Fair words are always plausible, and may mislead the ignorant, but all experience proves that you may as well speak of a well-regulated pandemonium as of a well-regulated bothy. . . . Landlords should be told plainly, and especially our Scotch landlords, that the very least thing they can do is to build decent cottages for those by the sweat of whose brows their rents are secured. . . . Either more attention must be paid to the social and moral elements in dealing with our working men, or we may prepare for a sweeping change by and by through the tempest of a revolution.'[20]

When the Social Science Association was formed and held its first annual meeting in 1857 at Birmingham under the presidency of Lord Brougham, Begg made a speech condemning the housing both in Edinburgh and Glasgow and in the agricultural districts of Scotland, and when, probably as a result, he read a paper next year at Liverpool on his favourite subject, the housing of the working classes including the bothy system, his revelations caused something of a sensation among the members. In this paper Begg affirmed, 'The system cannot be improved. It is essentially wrong. Anything that makes the family system impossible can only lead to evil, and that continually. The bothy system, therefore, must be extirpated and ploughmen allowed to marry, and this, we are persuaded, will require the strong hand of law. . . . The simplest and most effectual remedy would be to empower entailed proprietors to erect workmen's houses, and, failing this, all farmers to erect at once as many workmen's houses, consisting of at least two or three apartments, upon their farms as they require to employ ploughmen and labourers, and to retain the price when they pay their next rents. This would simply be an extension of a well-known principle that tenants are entitled to make necessary repairs and to charge the price to their landlords. It would probably remedy nine-tenths of the evil in two or three years and would only diminish the vast incomes of some of our large proprietors by the price of some unnecessary luxury.'[21] A few years later Begg was demanding government action 'to appoint authorized and paid public inspectors to examine all the cottages in the rural districts and to report to some magistrate who should have authority to order the redress of existing evils. . . . It might be said that the proposal in question implied a serious interference with the liberty of landlords to do what they would with their own estates. But the theory of liberty referred to, however plausible, had by universal consent been abandoned in regard to all other classes of the community. . . . Human selfishness and prejudice had always been too strong for mere remonstrance, and it was only when public opinion had assumed such an authoritative and commanding power as to be embodied in the action of the government that other social evils had been forced to give way.'[22]

In 1858 Begg began a strenuous campaign extending over nine years to awaken his own Church as well as the country generally to the seriousness of the housing situation. In the Free Church General Assembly of that year he brought forward an overture from the Synod of Lothian and Tweeddale on the subject, and in introducing it said that 'the Church had always been in the habit of affirming that the state of religion and morality had a most important bearing on the physical condition of the people; but he feared they had too long overlooked, as a Church court, the fact that the converse of the proposition was also true, that the physical state of the population had a most important bearing on the morality of the people'.[23] He asked for the appointment of a Committee to find the facts and lay them before the Assembly and he trusted that when they had them they would not scruple to bring the matter before the country and, if necessary, Parliament. A Committee was appointed with Begg as

Convener to inquire into the state of the dwellings of the working classes throughout Scotland, with special reference to the existence and extension of the bothy system, the bearings of this upon the morality of the people and the best means of securing a remedy for existing ills.

The successive annual reports of this Committee clearly showed the hand of the Convener, and the presentation of them to the General Assembly gave him scope to stress the valuable information gathered and to report progress. In 1859 he could claim that 'for the first time these social questions have bulked with anything like a due proportion to their intrinsic magnitude in our business' and could express the hope that in later years their place would become even more prominent.[24] The report to the Assembly of 1861 referred to the Committee's having been largely instrumental in getting inserted in the census form of that year a return of the number of rooms in every dwelling house. It is significant of the interest generated in Scotland that the question about the number of rooms was not inserted in the forms for England and Ireland. In his speech Begg referred to expectations of improvement in rural housing through the Act empowering landlords to build cottages and burden the estate with a large proportion of the cost. Previously Scottish landlords were forbidden by the law of entail to do this, and the Court of Session had decided that dog-kennels might be built, and a house for a man to look after the dogs might be provided, if needed, but not houses for ploughmen.[25] Begg and others persuaded Mr. Murray Dunlop, M.P., to introduce a bill to remedy this anomaly and it was passed in 1860. At this Assembly Begg told his fellow-ministers that 'if they wished to be benefactors to generations yet to come, they would not only preach the gospel faithfully, but would seek to arrest the progress of Satan's efforts and to cut up his plans by the root—they would seek to undo the heavy burdens and to teach masters to give unto their servants the things which are just and equal. That would make their Church a true and universal blessing in the land. . . .'[26]

The most outspoken and comprehensive report was that to the Assembly of 1862. It claimed that 'great progress has recently been made in promoting a much sounder public opinion in regard to the social state of the working classes. This, of course, must precede all action. The idea that Christian men and ministers have no interest in the question is almost entirely dispelled.' Some of the progress was doubtless due to an event which took place in November 1861 when an old tenement in the High Street of Edinburgh occupied by some thirty to forty families crashed, killing thirty-five persons and injuring a large number. Speaking of the difficulty of acquiring land for working men's houses as compared with the compulsory acquisition of land for streets and railways the report complained that 'according to the one-sided philosophy of certain writers, everything is fair and good so long as the interests of capitalists are involved, although it is manifestly done against the people—the sin only begins when you propose to do anything to promote their social elevation'.[27] One detects the indignant tones of Begg himself in the assertion that 'a spiritual canker has invaded many in all parts of the Protestant Church—not only the idea that the ministers of Christ have nothing to do with such so-called secular matters as the houses of the people, but that to manifest an utter indifference upon the whole subject is a mark of superior sanctity. To our mind this is not simply a reversal of the whole spirit of the Bible and the Reformation, it is a "glorying in our shame".' Municipal bodies, as well as sections of the Church, came in for rebuke—'can anyone remember when the houses of the people, their social and domestic comforts, and how to improve them, formed the subject of much discussion in any of our town councils?'[28]

While acknowledging progress in recent years both in public opinion and in actual improvements the report suggested that ministers and office-bearers should direct special attention to the subject; that masters who were members of the Church should be admonished to devote greater attention to the condition of their servants, and servants to fidelity and self-elevation; that all unnecessary restrictions on the acquisition of land should be removed; and that an attempt should be made to secure a Commission to examine the whole question of labourers' dwellings in Scotland. This last suggestion was taken up by the General Assembly. A petition was framed, embodying some of the facts and the evils proceeding from them, and asking for the appointment of a Royal Commission so that the whole facts should be ascertained and means of remedy be found. The petition was approved and appointed to be subscribed by the Moderator.[29]

The Committee's report for 1863 referred to the shocking facts revealed by the new question in the 1861 census paper. Of 666,786 houses in Scotland there were 7,964 without windows, and 226,723 houses of one apartment, which meant that about one million people, or nearly one-third of the entire population, were living in one-apartment houses. Not only so, but of these one-roomed houses 40,703 had each from 6 to 16 human beings residing in them. In Edinburgh there were 121 single-roomed houses without a window; there were 13,209 families, representing at least 50,000 of the population, living in houses of only one apartment, and of these one-roomed houses 1,530 had each from 6 to 15 inhabitants. In Glasgow there were 241 one-roomed houses without a window; and 28,269 houses with only one apartment each, containing a population of at least 100,000 : and of these one-roomed houses 2,212 had each from 7 to 15 inhabitants.

In 1866 the Committee reported gratifying tokens of advance such as the awakened interest of working people themselves in securing decent dwellings and the serious attention now being paid by civic authorities to the degraded state of parts of their cities; and it urged that 'whilst it is right to study all reasonable economy . . . a small assessment which may be necessary for social and sanitary purposes is never to be named in comparison with human life and human morality, whilst at the same time there is nothing ultimately so expensive as human degradation'.[30]

The final report of the Committee in 1867 was encouraging. It admitted that in rural areas much had been done of late years to build better cottages in some districts, but little had been done to remove the bothy and the farm-kitchen systems. Parliamentary investigation of these social evils was called for. Pointed reference was made to the one-third of the population living in houses of only one room, and it was declared that 'every Christian ought to consider how impossible it is that either decency or devotion can exist in such circumstances. . . . The reproach must be rolled away from the Church of Christ of supposed indifference to the temporal any more than to the spiritual interests of the people; and the social reformer and Christian minister must not only combine in seeking to alleviate and remove the desolations of many generations, but they must be combined in the same individuals.'[31]

This note of challenge and resolution was sounded because

the report stated—and here again the mind of Begg is evident—
that the problem was in principle solved. The Edinburgh Co-
operative Building Company was 'continually producing self-
contained working men's houses there, which are being bought
up by working men as fast as they are produced', and there were
similar ventures in other centres. It was triumphantly declared
that 'it is demonstrated beyond the possibility of a doubt that all
industrious and frugal working men can now obtain houses of
their own if they are only so disposed'.[32] The Committee, with
Begg's approval, was discharged as 'public attention was
thoroughly alive on the subject'.[33]

Begg's hopes for the solution of the housing problem were
centred on working men themselves who should be encouraged
to proceed by the method of co-operative building societies
supplemented by property-investment companies; and it must
be admitted that he had some reason to look expectantly in that
direction. He took a prominent part in advancing the most important and most enduring experiment in co-operative house-
building in Edinburgh, the Edinburgh Co-operative Building
Company, which was formed in April 1861 as the outcome of a
successful masons' strike for shorter hours. This enterprise was
planned and managed by the working men themselves. Its principles were co-operation and the use of a floating capital, that is
to say, instead of building to rent, it built to sell and build again.
Its aim was to make working men their own landlords, the members of the company having first choice of houses.

Begg had the honour of laying the foundation stone of the
Company's first row of houses at Stockbridge, Edinburgh, Reid
Terrace by name, in October 1861, and then of the second, Hugh
Miller Place, in 1862, and he was also one of the speakers on the
occasion of the laying of the foundation stone of houses at Haw-
thorn Bank, Leith, in March 1863.[34] By the time the National
Association for the Promotion of Social Science held its annual
meeting in 1863 it could be stated that 'in little more than two
years, and with a comparatively limited capital, 117 houses have
been erected or are in course of erection, at a value of more than
£17,000. The immediate object of the company is to build houses
suitable for working men, and sell them; but as the capital increases, the houses will be retained and let to the shareholders
or to others. Already 87 families have been comfortably supplied

and in the majority of cases the owner is the occupier, so that
we can say the houses have been planned by working men, built
by working men, bought by working men and tenanted by working men.'[35] Begg found three great obstacles to the progress of
this movement: the comparative want of sympathy with the
movement on the part of some of the higher ranks of society;
the difficulty and expense of getting titles to heritable property,
to overcome which he advocated a process of registration so
that the holding and transference of land and houses should be
as simple as the holding and selling of railway shares or other
securities; and most important, there was the difficulty of acquiring land on which houses might be erected. Here he invoked
the interposition of Parliament to enforce the principle that all
individual land rights were subordinate to the well-being of
society at large, and suggested that a certain width of land should
be set apart round every large town and should be acquirable in
perpetuity by the people for houses.[36]

Despite these difficulties the progress of the Edinburgh Co-
operative Building Company was such that interest in its proceedings appeared in distant and unexpected quarters. The
French Vice-consul at Leith approached Dr. Begg and asked for
detailed information about the aims and results of the enterprise,
and was furnished with plans, specifications and photographs of
the houses for transmission to the French government. About
the same time a similar inquiry was received from the Danish
Consul at Leith. Apparently a group of working men employed
by a firm at Copenhagen had formed a company to build good
and inexpensive houses for themselves. Their estimates of costs,
however, compared unfavourably with reports about the houses
built at Edinburgh and Leith. Accordingly they approached the
Danish Ministry of Foreign Affairs which through the Danish
Legation in London and the Consul at Leith inquired about the
rules of the Edinburgh Company and the specifications of its
houses.[37]

It is not surprising that Begg could feel that 'public attention
was thoroughly alive on the subject' of housing. That this judgment was altogether premature we know too well today. Indeed,
Begg himself must soon have realized that he had been too op-
timistic, for while in his later years he turned more to matters of
ecclesiastical controversy than previously, he continued to take

an interest in housing. In his address to the National Social Science Association meeting in Glasgow in 1874, as in the report of his Church Committee in 1867, he had to admit that, while considerable improvements had taken place, much was far from satisfactory still. 'The "bondager system", as it is called, still exists in some parts of the border counties; the "bothy" system is widely prevalent in certain districts; the "farm kitchen" system obtains in other quarters; whilst the houses of the miners and colliers are sometimes very defective. . . . It is never economical to do wrong, and it is less economical in the long run to ill-use men than to ill-use cattle.' Again he called for a Royal Commission to investigate social conditions in the rural areas, and he pictured his practicable aim thus: 'We do not justify unreasonable complaints, but we cannot see why every ploughman might not have a good cottage, with two or three apartments and a rood of land for a garden. If he were encouraged to become owner of his cottage, and if he had a cow, as in some parts of East Lothian, so much the better for all parties.'[38]

On the same occasion Begg gave a further report on the Edinburgh Co-operative Building Company which, he said, was managed entirely by working men. Its capital was £10,000 in shares of £1 each. By means of this sum continually turned over it had built, by October 1872, 914 houses which had been readily sold, chiefly to working men, and these men had been able to redeem them in fourteen years at a rate very little exceeding the rent which they would have paid as tenants during the same period. The houses were self-contained, each of from three to five apartments, with every convenience and with a small garden. His ideal for the city working man is revealed in this passage— 'all the professed patronage of working men in cities as if they required to have amusements provided for them, and were a kind of children incapable of managing their own affairs, and requiring to have houses provided for them by charity whilst they waste their money in noxious indulgences, should utterly cease. Beyond giving them good advice and helping them to help themselves, especially by labouring to remove obstacles which stand in their way, the interposition of the higher classes is not required, and is only mischievous.'[39] Again at a large meeting held in the City Hall of Glasgow in January 1875 Begg gave an address which was published as *The Health and Homes of Work-*

ing People. He reasserted his Scriptural authority for dealing with social questions like housing and adduced the facts and arguments which had been his stock-in-trade for a quarter of a century. Their appositeness may be judged from some figures presented by the Lord Provost of Glasgow who presided at the meeting. From these it appeared that there were in the city 110,258 houses, of which 35,583 were of one apartment and housed 167,918 persons, while there were 47,781 of two apartments, housing 223,258 persons. Thus in 83,365 houses of one or two apartments there lived 391,176 persons, or three-quarters of the population of the city at that time.

It is particularly regrettable to have to record that Begg's sanguine expectations that the problem would be solved by working men's co-operative building societies were not realized. The Edinburgh Company with which he was associated seems all too soon to have lost its original co-operative character; for, while the Royal Commission during the First World War reported that the Edinburgh Co-operative Building Company had in the course of a little over fifty years built 2,080 houses, it added: 'We do not, however, propose to give an account of its operations, as it has for many years ceased to provide houses within the means even of the better-paid artisans.'[40] This Commission mentions several such societies started shortly after the Edinburgh one—at Falkirk, Hawick, Dumbarton and Grangemouth —and states that each had erected about ten houses a year, but adds that more than one had slowed down its operations or altogether stopped in the early years of the present century. Hence the Commissioners, while declaring that this movement had set a better standard of housing in some of the Scots burghs and that it should be encouraged in every way possible, nevertheless summed up thus: 'From the evidence before us we conclude that these societies, while taking a considerable part in a number of towns in providing working-class houses of a satisfactory kind, have not contributed very largely in the provision of such houses throughout Scotland.'[41]

A memorial of James Begg's interest in housing remains in Edinburgh in the form of a block of tenements at Abbeyhill, facing the King's Park, which still bears prominently upon it the title of Begg's Buildings, as he laid the foundation stone. The proprietor was Robert Cranston, an ex-Chartist leader and a temperance-hotel owner. He enacted certain by-laws for the guidance of his tenants and provided them with a washing-house. The buildings are five stories in height and consist of two-apartment dwellings. In 1860 they were mentioned with other similar enterprises in Edinburgh in a paper read at a meeting of the National Association for the Promotion of Social Science at its annual conference in Glasgow, and were criticized on two grounds—'defective in some important conveniences and the passages are very narrow'.[42]

In all his work for better housing Begg insisted that efforts for improving the dwellings and elevating the character of the poor must go together. There could be no morality, he urged, without decent dwellings. He was more disposed than most of his contemporaries to advocate better housing as a means of improving the standard of morality. His own statement of the philosophy behind his housing zeal is contained in the preface to his *Happy Homes for Working Men* (1866), where he lays down the general principle 'that the family system, like the Sabbath law, being an institution of Paradise, is essentially connected with the permanent well-being of man. No mere extension of barrack accommodation will therefore cure the evil which exists. Man must not only have a covering, but a HOME. God made men in families; and it is upon the right maintenance and ordering of these little kingdoms that the peace and social order of all the great kingdoms of the world depends. . . .'[43] His ideal was a property-owning Christian democracy. 'It may be affirmed with certainty,' he wrote, 'that whilst all experience proves that nothing but Christian principle will give a steady elevation to the human character, the possessory feeling, within certain limits, is powerful for good, whilst degrading social arrangements are always the ministers of vice.' On the other hand he never supposed that the regeneration of human society could proceed 'from the mere multiplication of comfortable dwellings, apart from the fear and grace of God. It is a vast step in advance, no doubt, to secure such dwellings—probably by far the greatest that can be secured by mere material means; but the multiplication of Bethels—houses in which the fear and worship of God shall be found—is what we really want.'[44]

Besides housing Begg advocated many other objects for the benefit of the working classes. In the interests of a property-owning democracy he took a leading part in the unsuccessful campaign for the extension to Scotland of the forty-shilling free-holder franchise. For centuries the forty-shilling freeholder in England had enjoyed the parliamentary franchise, but not in Scotland. Begg believed that the institution of such a franchise would stimulate the working classes to acquire small lots of land and thus attain comparative independence. He also supported the early closing of shops and at a meeting in Edinburgh moved a motion voicing the opinion 'that the curtailment of the hours of business is quite practicable, and will never operate against the interests of the employer nor cause inconvenience to the public'.[45] He held enlightened views on recreation and was proud to claim that it was to him that the people of Edinburgh owed their free access to East Princes Street Gardens. To him this was a matter of principle. 'Cities,' he declared, 'are necessary; but men were never made to be pent up in unbroken and feverish masses. And since every family in a city cannot have a garden of its own, the next best thing is to have public gardens, in which a man with his children may spend a portion of his leisure, and breathe the pure air of heaven. . . . Man must have recreation. . . . The only question is, Shall it be innocent or sinful?'[46]

Begg's social concern went far beyond Scotland. At the General Assembly of the Free Church in 1859 he introduced an overture from the Presbytery of Edinburgh calling upon the Assembly to remonstrate with the Government about the opium trade. 'They were responsible for the proceedings of their rulers, at least in so far as they allowed them to do evil without lifting up their protest against their proceedings', which in connexion with 'this trade were of such a kind as earnestly to call for the strenuous remonstrance of all Christian men'. It was unanimously agreed to appoint a Committee with power to memoralize the queen and to petition both houses of Parliament against the complicity of their country in such guilt.[47]

Begg had a deep sympathy with the common people and great gifts as a popular speaker. He was something of a demagogue and occasionally used his powers in a way that was unfair to opponents. Nevertheless he deserves grateful remembrance for his social zeal. Though he was conservative by temperament, in social matters he held many radical opinions, and declared them fearlessly in season and out of season.

9

THE SCOTTISH CHURCH AND EDUCATION

THE Scottish Reformers believed wholeheartedly in the education of both old and young, and proposed that the support of a comprehensive scheme of education should be a charge on the patrimony of the Kirk. The continued existence of the Reformed Church depended on the planting of schools as well as the planting of kirks, for it was only by moulding the outlook of each successive generation and making it familiar with the Scriptures that loyalty to the Reformed Faith could be maintained and the youth of the land be brought up to the service of God and the commonweal. It was no accident therefore that Knox and Melville, following the example of Calvin, were educationists as well as churchmen, and that the *First Book of Discipline* was more than any other document responsible for the ideal of education that persisted in Scotland down to the latter part of the nineteenth century.

Knox's plans in the *Book of Discipline* were patriotic and statesmanlike, but the patrimony of the Kirk had become the prey of nobles and landowners who had plans of their own for it. Moreover, to begin with at any rate the Reformed Church could not have provided sufficient schoolmasters, though many ministers did what they could by conducting schools in their parishes.[1] One must confess that Knox's scheme, wonderfully enlightened as it was, never came to more in the sixteenth, seventeenth, and eighteenth centuries than an outline of what might have been. The records of the Church courts show the Church's zeal for the establishment of schools, for the trial and inspection of schoolmasters and indeed for a measure of pressure on parents, rich and poor alike, to get them to send their children to school.[2] Ineffective as this zeal may have been over large parts of the country, it did bring it about in the Lowland counties that many people, who could not write, could at least read, that the Bible, which was the main text-book of the school, became also the

main reading of the home, and the Scots became in a real sense
a people of that one Book.

The acceptance by the State of the Church's ideal of a school
and schoolmaster for every parish is first made clear in a decree
of the Privy Council in 1616, which required that a school should
be established and a fit person appointed as teacher in every
parish 'when convenient means may be had', a phrase which left
an obvious loophole. There were several Acts of Parliament to
the same effect during the troublous times of the seventeenth
century, but the great Act for Settling of Schools did not come
till 1696. It declared that the heritors in every parish should provide a commodious house for a school and settle and modify a
salary to a schoolmaster and assess themselves for these purposes. This was virtually a repetition of an Act of 1646; but it
contained a provision, calculated to make it more effective, that
presbyteries might call in the county commissioners of supply if
the heritors neglected to fulfil the part assigned to them. Other
Acts passed in succeeding generations gave statutory authority to
what doubtless generally prevailed in practice—that the superintendence of the parish schools was in the hands of the parish
minister, that the schoolmaster, after his election by the heritors,
should be examined by the presbytery and should sign the Confession of Faith and the formula of the Church of Scotland. Thus
the national establishment included a school and a schoolmaster,
as well as a minister and a church, in every parish. Alas, this ideal
took a long time to find realization. In 1719 we find the General
Assembly appointing presbyteries, where schools are lacking in
parishes, to set the legal machinery in motion to get the Act
made effectual. Even drastic action of that sort often failed to
attain its end. In 1758 there were still 175 parishes without a
parochial school. The Presbytery of Ayr is an instance: in 1735
there were twelve parishes which had 'no school provyded nor a
sallary to a schoolmaster according to law, and have taken instruments against their heritors for not doing it.' In 1752 there was
still no school at Auchinleck, and in 1758 still none at New
Cumnock.[3]

In the Highlands especially schools were sadly few; but the
situation was to a notable extent relieved by the Society in
Scotland for Propagating Christian Knowledge. Founded in
1709, it had by 1732 provided 'English schools' in 109 parishes,

and from 1738 onwards it was authorized to establish spinning-schools for girls too. By 1748 it had 134 schools with 5,187 boys and 2,618 girls enrolled.[4] Dr. Archibald Main sums up the eighteenth century thus: 'The conclusion seems inevitable. The Church had failed to realize the ideal which it had set before itself since the days of John Knox. There was no uniform system of education throughout the parishes. In some places there were efficient schools and schoolmasters; in others, even when there was a school, the master was a student who had failed to reach the ministry of the Church, or a man who had but a smattering of knowledge, or a poor dependant of a heritor, or a soldier who had returned from foreign wars. . . . The poverty of the Church and of many heritors in the eighteenth century, the social and economic circumstances of the era, a lack of imagination on the part of many ministers, some lukewarmness regarding the nobility of the teaching profession in the parish schools, and perhaps an undue regard for a narrow theological discipline—such were some of the considerations which prevented a widespread system of sound elementary education in every parish of Scotland.'[5] Yet along with much that was unsatisfactory, there was also solid achievement, as seems clear from the first Statistical Account; and a more recent authority states that, 'Since at the close of the century only ten parishes in all Scotland were without a school, it can be said that, though there were wide variations from one parish to another in teaching, attendance, accommodation and remuneration, the ideal laid down by Knox in 1560 had at last been broadly realized.'[6]

By this time, however, there were many private schools. Anyone could start a school, subject to a vague right of supervision by the local Presbytery; and with the growth of wealth and population in the eighteenth century not a few were started. The surprising result followed that by the end of the Napoleonic wars twice as many children in Scotland were receiving some kind of education in private schools as in the parochial schools. George Lewis summarizes the situation as revealed by the Report of the Education and Charity Commissioners in 1816: 'In the whole of Scotland there were 942 parish schools; that is little more than one to each parish. Private schools had sprung up to the number of 2,222, twice the number of parish schools; and the attendance at schools of all sorts over Scotland did not exceed 176,303, that

is, not above one-twelfth of the entire population was at school in
1816.'[7] With this estimate there is substantial agreement in parliamentary papers of 1820, based on a survey by a Committee of
the General Assembly reporting in 1818. The unfavourable impression made by such figures is intensified when attention is
directed to certain parts of the country. The General Assembly's
Committee had been inquiring into the management of the poor
in Scotland, and reported that while no deficiency of the means
of common education was apparent in the Lowland Synods, it
was very different in the Highlands. In Tongue, for instance, out
of a population of 2,400 there were 1,200 not taught, while in
the Presbytery of Uist, in one parish not more than three or four
hundred out of a population of five thousand could read, and in
another but few persons had been taught.[8] In the Lowlands,
however, the Church's stress on Bible and Catechism brought it
about that many who could not write could read, for to be unable to read was a greater disgrace than to be unable to write.[9]

In the post-Waterloo period there was a decided quickening
of interest in education. In 1824 the General Assembly appointed
a Committee on Education, which has become its oldest standing
committee, and charged it with the task of co-ordinating provision for Church Schools. The following year the Committee
began to establish and support what were known as Assembly
Schools, as distinct from Sessional Schools which were supported by individual kirk-sessions. The Committee set up some
eighty schools in the Highlands and Islands between 1824 and
1835, and by 1843 there were 146 Assembly Schools with an
enrolment of 13,000. A notable example of the Sessional School
was that known as St. George's Institution, begun in 1823 by
Dr. Andrew Thomson with the co-operation of his kirk-session
and numerous friends for the benefit of the children of St.
George's Parish, Edinburgh. A kirk-session sometimes took a
smaller but a not unimportant part in encouraging the desire for
education. In a large parish a group of parents, in a district
remote from the parish school, would put their purses together
and engage as schoolmaster some needy student who would be
glad of board and lodging in the summer months and a few
pounds in his pocket to help him through his winter studies at
the University. In the Session minutes of Kirkpatrick-Juxta
there is the following entry: 'October 20, 1818. Granted Robert

Flint to assist the Dumgree School this year, £1.' This Robert Flint was grandfather of the Professor of that name, and there is evidence that the teacher of this school lodged with the Flint family.[10] Through such measures on the larger or smaller scale the number of children attending school increased, but, with the population also increasing, it is probable that the proportion of literate to illiterate remained much as before.

The great figure of Thomas Chalmers must come into the picture here, for his scheme for the Christian good of Scotland involved not only the division of parishes and the provision of many new churches but also a school or schools attached to each new church, as his own vigorous example in St. John's Parish goes to prove. It was not alone, however, the enthusiasm for education of the great preacher which gave the impulse towards educational experimentation and progress which came chiefly from Glasgow in the third and fourth decades of the nineteenth century. There was another factor of immense importance—the practical idealism of a Christian business man who loved children, and whose 'enlightened and single-minded devotion to the cause of education' achieved results both far-reaching and abiding.[11]

David Stow, son of a Paisley merchant, was born in 1793 and went to Glasgow in 1811 to join a commercial firm. It was his daily custom to walk from his home on the south side of the River Clyde through the Saltmarket to his place of business, and so he became aware of the overcrowding, filth and moral degradation in that part of the city. A piece of voluntary work—the distribution of funds for a society for the relief of destitute old men —gave him a fuller insight into social conditions and convinced him that the old were practically hopeless and that he must make his reforming experiments with the young.[12] At first he spoke to children anywhere he encountered them; but he soon saw that he must confine himself to a definite locality and penetrate beyond the streets into the depths of the dwellings. He chose a densely populated part of the Saltmarket where two lanes held some seventy families. These lanes he visited twice a week till he got to know the background and circumstances of every family and the name of every child. From these families he gathered about thirty boys and girls in a room and taught them the Bible. That Sunday evening school in the Saltmarket in 1816 was the humble beginning of an educational system which still has its influence today. It was too from such work begun by Stow that Chalmers learned the possibilities of the 'local system', as against the plan of gathering children to a school irrespective of where they lived. Together they increased the number of local Sunday Schools by enlisting voluntary helpers to take charge. An ardent supporter was William Collins, already an elder with Chalmers, as Stow also became in 1821. Collins was a believer in Sunday Schools and in day schools for the poor, and had opened a Sunday School in his own house in the autumn of 1815, and had begun to spread a chain of Sunday Schools throughout the district. By 1817 upwards of twelve hundred children were under regular instruction in the Tron parish.[13]

Encouraged by Chalmers the Sunday School movement spread; but Stow saw that this was not enough. Six days' exposure to the evils of the slums was not to be counteracted by an hour's teaching on the Sabbath evening. A day school was necessary, and one that would impart habit-formation as well as head knowledge. Stow received many lessons in his first experiment in the room in the Saltmarket. After much disappointment and failure he learned how to handle children and what could be done with them, and thereby gained the leading principles of his training system. The beginning was far from auspicious. The room was a kitchen. Stow brought in his crowd of urchins and set them down and bowed his head for prayer. The candles went out, and by the time he had lit them again, he was alone. Without any complaint he patiently went on visiting the families till he had won back his pupils. That he was a born teacher is evident. One restless, ragged and barefoot boy was prominent as a trouble-maker. He sat on the third seat from the front, and taking a long pin between his toes, he watched his chance and stabbed at the bare feet and legs in front. The result was pandemonium. Stow, being opposed to corporal punishment, neither stormed at the boy nor punished nor expelled him, but pointed out to him the pain he had caused. A little later he put him in charge of the candles, making him responsible for snuffing them. The boy became one of his keenest pupils.[14] Thus Stow saw beyond the rags and dirt and indiscipline to the sensitive, inquiring minds of the children and their moral possibilities. In fact he loved them and won their love in return. Yet he could claim no spectacular results. During ten years of work in that kitchen in the Saltmarket he saw little fruit of his labour, except, as he put it, 'that they all got better and more decently dressed, and their hair more smoothly combed or brushed, and that several of them attended church, and whose parents were now induced to attend, who had never done so before.'[15]

This however, did not satisfy Stow. His aim was that children should grow up properly developed persons, not merely more orderly and decent. Education, he believed, must be continuous and systematic; and he began to perceive principles which he was to use in later years and to proclaim in his books and addresses: no corporal punishment, no prizes, no place-taking; the sympathy of numbers more effective than corporal punishment; picturing out in words instead of mechanical repetition; and the use of the playground to reverse the training of the streets.[16] It ought to be added that there were other pioneers in the field at this period. The experiments of Wood in Edinburgh were known, though Stow believed that they put too much stress on intellectual development to the neglect of moral training. Bell and Lancaster had spread a form of education among the poorer classes in England largely by means of the monitorial system. Robert Owen's infant school attached to the cotton mill at New Lanark had drawn attention, partly because of Owen's religious scepticism. Samuel Wilderspin was pioneering the opening of infant schools in London and his methods, including the use of gallery and playground, must have been known to Stow.

As soon as Stow came out into the open with his views and suggestions he was confronted with all the self-satisfaction of the Scottish educational tradition as well as the complacency of those who did not realize the evils to be remedied. Nevertheless the outcome was the formation in 1826 of the Glasgow Infant School Society, with Stow as associate secretary. A day school was set up in a house with a garden in the Drygate in the spring of 1827. There was room for about a hundred pupils, for a dwelling-house for the teacher, and for facilities for training a few students for extending the new system elsewhere. The garden became the playground, and the upper floor of the house was cleared out and a gallery erected.[17] The Bible was the basis of all instruction; but the methods by which the schoolmaster, at Stow's direction, sought to impart the truths of Scripture were novel—not merely intellectual instruction, far less learning by rote, but moral training, by stimulating the child to a response in classroom and playground. Like all educational reformers of the day Stow believed in, 'Train up a child in the way he should go: and when he is old he will not depart from it'; but he wanted to begin that training earlier than most, as early as two or three and not later than six years of age. His aim was not only to provide moral training in connexion with elementary instruction but also to form the characters of the children of vicious parents before their environment had moulded their natural propensities into evil habits. He hoped to see infant schools extended throughout the land, and all schools—parochial, adventure or sessional—making use of gallery and playground and carrying out the teaching methods of his system.

For a time the Infant School excited wide interest. Groups of the pupils were taken to other towns to give demonstrations and were enthusiastically welcomed. The outcome, however, was disappointing, for the venture was on too small and limited a scale to convince the public that Stow's ideas could be applied through the whole range of education. Interest and subscriptions began to fall away till Stow was left almost alone; but he was not thereby deterred from taking over larger premises in the Saltmarket. In 1830, too, he bought land for a playground behind St. John's Parish School and was allowed to fit up the already existing classrooms according to his own ideas. This enabled him to show what he could do with children over six years of age, of whom he soon had two hundred in what could be called a Model Juvenile Training School. Students came at their own expense to study his methods, and some became enthusiastic converts and carried news of the new methods far and wide, even beyond Scotland, so that the distinction between teaching and training, the importance of the playground or 'uncovered school' and the necessity for the training of teachers began to be recognized by informed opinion.[18] The playground, though often misunderstood by observers, was an essential part of the training. It was not simply a place for fresh-air and exercise in the interests of health. It was a sphere for active training in such virtues as self-restraint and courtesy, and Stow demanded that his teachers should participate in all the games and other activities. Whether inside or outside the great aim was not merely instruction but the stimulating of the child to an active response and the guiding of his activities by a mature and cultured mind.

A notable supporter was the Rev. George Lewis, for some years editor of the *Scottish Guardian* and later minister of St. David's, Dundee, who in 1834 reconstituted the Infant School Society as the Glasgow Educational Society, becoming himself Joint-Secretary with Stow. In 1835 the Society took over the Model Schools which Stow had been maintaining at his own charges, for it intended to apply the improved methods, which Stow had worked out, to the parochial schools at large, and it hoped to achieve this by way of teacher training.[19] Like other societies of the day it began by issuing pamphlets. The first, written by Lewis, came out in 1834 with the startling title, *Scotland a Half-Educated Nation, both in the quantity and quality of her Educational Institutions.* It was a masterly survey of the position in Scotland and included a comparison with other countries well calculated to shatter traditional complacency. We have already quoted a summary of the figures as they stood in 1816, whereby it appeared that the attendance at schools of all sorts in Scotland did not exceed one-twelfth of the population. Lewis declared that 'every child between six and fourteen, allowing for sickness, ought to be at school to ensure universal and efficient education',[20] and he estimated that to cover all the children between these ages it would be necessary to have not one-twelfth but one-fifth of the population at school. Scotland was lagging far behind such countries as Prussia, France, and certain parts of America. It would not be sufficient, however, merely to increase the quantity of education. Quality was also important, and the first step, said Lewis, was 'the establishment of normal schools or seminaries for teaching the teachers of youth. That every profession, save the difficult one of schoolmaster, should have its apprenticeship will appear some fifty years hence a singular fact in the history of the educational institutions of Europe.'[21]

Lewis had also enlightened ideas, doubtless derived from Stow, about educational methods. 'We trust ere long a series of pictures of objects of natural history and a small museum of minerals and metals will become as necessary an appendage to every school as books and slates and forms at present are.'[22] What Lewis had in view was a national system of schools with teacher-training colleges, all financed by parish rates and central grants, but locally under the control of the Church, represented by the minister and kirk-session in every parish. Regarding the expense, Lewis declared roundly, 'if the nation will not pay for the schoolmaster to prevent crime, it must pay tenfold for the repression of social disorder, and for coercing an unhappy, dissolute and reckless population.'[23] Among other incentives to action was the patriotic one. 'In all but our parochial churches and parochial schools we have lost our nationality. In these alone we survive as a nation—stand apart from and superior to England.'[24]

Another incentive to the educational reformers of the early nineteenth century—Chalmers, Stow, Lewis, Collins, and others —was the safeguarding of the peace and stability of society. Fear of revolutionary outbreaks like the French Revolution was widespread till the middle of the century, and it was commonly held that the great antidote was a Bible education. Thus, the aim of education, as far as the town masses at any rate were concerned, was rather moral discipline than the mere training of the mind. Education must involve the production of the good citizen and the only education capable of doing that was an education in which the Bible predominated. That would not mean, according to Stow, that the Bible should be the chief ordinary lessonbook; but it would mean that the teacher should be a person of Christian character, deeply versed in the Bible, and that, while religious services should be restricted to specified times, biblical illustrations and biblical precepts should be used at any time.

While the Glasgow Educational Society aimed at awakening Scotland to its educational shortcomings, with a view to a great extension and improvement of the parochial schools under the Church, it knew that for the realization of that aim the aid of Parliament was necessary. Accordingly it prepared a petition to the House of Commons, but in the meantime it turned to a matter that was more within its own powers—the establishment of a Normal College for the training of teachers, with four Model Schools, Initiatory, Junior, Senior, and a School of Industry for girls, including seventeen classrooms, two teachers' houses and large playgrounds. When completed the scheme would afford accommodation for the training of a hundred teachers and the education of a thousand children. The Treasury was asked for a building grant; but when, after fourteen months, nothing was forthcoming, it was decided to proceed with part of the scheme.

On 14 November 1836 the foundation stone of the Normal College at Dundas Vale, Glasgow, the first in Britain, was laid by Mr. J. C. Colquhoun, M.P., President of the Society, and the new institution was opened in the autumn of 1837. The College was at once successful in attracting students from Scotland and beyond. The Wesleyan Conference Education Committee sent its students for training for a number of years till it had established its own College in London, where it installed Glasgow-trained teachers. Visitors were welcomed, and among those who bore witness to the value of the training provided was Dr. Kay, later Sir James Kay-Shuttleworth, who was to play a major part in the development of education in England. Financially, however, the situation was difficult, for there was a debt of nearly £11,000 on the buildings. A small beginning of national financial aid to education had been made in 1834 when the Government sanctioned grants for school buildings through religious bodies. Accordingly a plea was made for £5,000 for the College buildings and £500 a year for maintenance. Sir James Kay-Shuttleworth, Secretary of the Privy Council Committee, was favourable; but the condition was laid down that the directors of the Society should transfer the property to the Church of Scotland. Stow did not see any necessity for this, but he yielded, only to find that he and other individual members of the Glasgow Educational Society were left responsible for the balance of debt outstanding, amounting to over £5,000.

Hard upon this came the Disruption, when Stow and his associates with one exception, and all the teachers of the Normal College with one exception, joined the Free Church.[25] Stow had no desire to found another College, and would have been glad to carry on the existing institution as a national agency for the training of teachers of any denomination. The Church of Scotland, however, chose to exercise its rights, and the Free Church felt itself obliged to set up two Normal Colleges, in Glasgow and Edinburgh, as the counterpart of the two institutions now belonging to the Established Church—that begun in Glasgow in 1837 and the other begun in Edinburgh shortly before the Disruption. Thus by 1845 there was good provision for teacher training in four Normal Colleges; but in other respects the quickened interest in education, manifest in the years just after the Reform Bill, had failed to produce much improvement.

Apart from some money grants begun in 1834, no State action took place. The Government was not alive to the importance of the matter, and with the Voluntaries and Radicals watchful over anything that might seem to favour the Established Church, it was bound to refuse financial support for such a scheme as Lewis had outlined—a scheme leaving control in the hands of the Church of Scotland. The breaking of the unity of that Church in 1843 need not have made much difference, for the Free Church had sufficient burdens to carry without going in for a system of schools. When, however, the Established Church used its powers and influence to oust teachers who connected themselves with the Free Church, the result was that some 400 teachers were out of employment for whom the Free Church felt itself morally responsible, and a system of Free Church Schools was initiated with remarkable success. In 1850 Dr. Candlish 'reported the establishment of 657 subsidized schools with an attendance in them of close upon 60,000 pupils. There were, however, a number of other Free Church Schools which derived no support from the Committee, and when these were taken account of, the calculation was that about 74,000 children were receiving education at the hands of the Free Church.'[26]

The growth of Free Church Schools made the Scottish educational pattern more manifold than ever. There were now some nine or ten types of school: the old parochial schools; the burgh schools, mostly under town councils and concerned chiefly with secondary education; the parliamentary schools, dating from 1838, in which the salary was provided by the State when in *quoad sacra* parishes the heritors built school and schoolhouse; the sessional schools, of which there were about one hundred, mostly in urban centres; the Assembly Schools; the Free Church Schools; the Society schools, mostly in the Highlands; other Church schools such as United Presbyterian, Roman Catholic, Episcopal; philanthropic schools of various kinds, for example, ragged schools, reformatory schools, schools of industry; and finally private schools, either privately endowed or pure adventure schools.

Thus by the middle of the century it was beginning to be clear to all that the only authority capable of unifying the country's education was the State, and that education would never be either satisfactory or universal unless it could also be under a national compulsory State scheme. Between 1849 and 1872 no less than ten education bills were brought before Parliament. The principles of these bills were the same; central and local supervision, inspection and compulsory rating, and they all, with the exception of one in 1861 which abolished the religious tests hitherto imposed on parochial teachers, came to grief on the question of religious instruction under a state system.

Meantime, the trend of educational policy was away from the enlightened ideas of David Stow. It was his policy to place pupils of the same age and of approximately uniform attainments under one master. Monitors were thus unnecessary, and when the numbers became too large for one teacher, an assistant was appointed. He demanded the best teachers possible for all grades. Hardly, however, had the Free Church Normal College in Glasgow got under way than there were issued certain Minutes of the Privy Council which, being based on the educational system of England, introduced into Scotland the pupil-teacher system which was destined to persist in this country for sixty years. Stow opposed the employment of inexperienced pupil-teachers and continued to demand qualified masters with trained assistants. He also strongly objected to entrusting to pupil-teachers the superintendence of the children's activities in the playground. The Minutes of Council also had the effect of changing the nature of the Normal Training Colleges. They became in effect institutions for completing the education of the pupil-teachers. Since the students had to prepare for examinations on which the money value of their certificates depended, they had less time and attention to bestow on the philosophy, principles and methods of training. Hence Stow was impelled to urge the establishment of separate preparatory colleges where the education demanded by the government for certificated teachers should be given, after which the students should pass to the Training Colleges proper. If instruction and training must be in the same institution then he pleaded for three years as the minimum course —two years in the preparatory classes and one year afterwards exclusively confined to the practical work of intellectual and moral training. Needless to say these views were not adopted by the authorities. Then in 1862 came the Revised Code which provided that H.M. Inspectors should make an annual examination, in the three Rs, of all the pupils individually in the primary classes of state-aided schools. Here again Stow found his principles being violated; for the inevitable result was that in the natural anxiety of the teacher to secure results for the inspector's eye the mechanical aspect of education became dominant and the moral character of the school as a training-ground fell into insignificance.[27]

As we have seen, the necessity of a national system of education had become clear by the middle of the century, if it had not indeed been so twenty years earlier. Unfortunately the problem of religious instruction under the projected system caused delay for another twenty years. There was a secularist party who would give no place to religion in the curriculum. The Church of Scotland stood firmly for the definite prescription by law of the continued teaching of Bible and Catechism. The Free Church also desired that some security for religious teaching should be provided. The United Presbyterian Church had taken up the position in 1847 that the duty of religious training belonged to the parents and the Church, not the State; and some interpreted that to mean a purely secular education. In 1869, however, that Church's Synod adopted the position that it would offer no objection if the people of any parish agreed to the applying of State funds to religious education. This statement was made in the light of the Report of a Royal Commission under the Duke of Argyll which reviewed Scottish education between 1864 and 1867 and reported that the parochial system, even with the help of denominational and private schools of every kind, was inadequate, more especially in the Highlands and Islands, and that nothing short of a national system would suffice. It appeared that 1 in 6·5 of the population was on a school roll and 1 in 7·9 was in attendance; but an analysis of these figures in detail was much less satisfactory, for the proportion in individual parishes varied from 1 in 4 to 1 in 15, 20, 25 or even 30.[28] In Glasgow the schools of all descriptions supplied accommodation for less than one half of the children of school age; but little more than one-third of the children of that age were in fact attending school.[29] It was also estimated that there were 92,000 children in the whole country not attending any school.[30] The voluntary system was clearly inadequate. Moreover, while a 'very large amount of substantial and efficient education' was provided by the voluntary efforts of the Established and Free Churches and by undenominational schools, the efficiency was 'very unequal', and the private adventure schools were condemned as 'almost invariably detrimental both to the health and education of all the children who attend them'.[31] It appeared that the situation of the school and the merits of the teacher weighed much more than religious differences in determining the school which children attended.[32] 'The defects in the present system are want of organization, want of supervision by some competent central authority powerful enough to make its influence felt by every individual connected with it, and want of thoroughness in the matter of teaching.'[33] Scotland was ripe for a national system.

Not till 1872 was the Act passed which gave statutory authority to the two great principles that suitable education must be provided for every child of school age in the land and that every child was bound to take advantage of the education provided. In particular the Act provided for compulsory attendance between the ages of five and thirteen, school boards elected triennially in all parishes to provide the elementary school accommodation required—in the first instance by taking over the parish and the parliamentary schools and by accepting the transfer of others. Public elementary schools were to be supported by rates levied by the school boards and by Government grants, and all aided schools were to be inspected. No real help was given to secondary education, and it was at that point that the ladder from primary school to University remained most deficient. It was left open to school boards to continue religious instruction, subject to the right of parents to withdraw their children under a conscience clause.

Almost to the last the Church of Scotland opposed the Bill because it did not guarantee religious instruction. Something, however, was done to meet this point by the introduction into the preamble to the Bill of a phrase giving a prescriptive right to 'use and wont'—'and whereas it has been the custom in the public schools of Scotland to give instruction in religion to children whose parents did not object to the instruction so given . . . and it is expedient that the managers of public schools shall be at liberty to continue the said custom. . . .'[34] In practice it was found that the school boards, reflecting the views of the public, continued the teaching of Bible and Catechism, subject to the conscience clause.

Under the Act school boards were authorized to accept voluntary transfers of schools, other than the parochial schools, but not to make any payment for them. Accordingly, many of the schools belonging to the Presbyterian Churches were at once transferred, and the remainder, continuing to receive grants if considered as contributing efficiently to the education of the parish or burgh where they were set, gradually ceased to exist over the ensuing half-century. In 1867 there were 519 Church of Scotland schools: of these 118 were transferred, and of the remaining 401, 145 were still receiving grants in 1880, but by 1910 the number had dwindled to 8. Similarly, there were 617 Free Church schools in 1867, of which 162 were transferred. Of the remaining 455, 39 were receiving grants in 1880 but by 1910 only one. On the other hand the Roman Catholic and Episcopalian schools tended to increase. Of 74 Episcopalian schools in 1867, 8 were transferred; but 73 such schools were receiving grants in 1880, and the number was still 57 in 1910. Of 61 Roman Catholic schools in 1867 only one was transferred, but Roman Catholic schools receiving grants in 1880 numbered 126, and in 1910, 220. Undenominational schools in 1867 numbered 1,084. Of these 301 were transferred. Of the remainder there were 235 receiving grants in 1880, and in 1910 only 61.[35]

According to the Act of 1872 the school boards were to take over the election of teachers as well as the management of the schools, and they were to supersede the town councils, heritors and parish ministers with respect to obligations and duties toward the public schools. All jurisdiction, power, and authority exercised by Presbyteries or other Church courts over public schools in Scotland were abolished. The Church had lost its control of education; yet that did not at first make much difference to religious instruction, all the more since it did not apply to the Normal Training Colleges, and the teachers continued to be trained in these Church institutions. In his report for 1878 one of H.M. Inspectors of Schools said, 'The boards, with surprising uniformity of action, or rather inaction, practically left the subject in the position in which they found it. They simply stereotyped and enforced the hereditary *status quo*, or what is termed "use and wont". The mass of the Scotch people are Presbyterians, and for these the national schools may be said to exist, just as the Roman Catholic and Episcopal schools respectively exist for these denominations. The public schools are to all intents and purposes denominational schools. Public and Presbyterian are practically interchangeable terms. Inspection is, perhaps, after all the only really undenominational feature in our educational arrangements. But the system is said to work well. Everybody is pleased, and the religious difficulty is solved.'[36]

Thus it seemed as if the dreams of John Knox were at long last to be fully realized, as if what the Church had tried to do within the limits of its powers was now to be done universally by the State. Yet there was a difference of emphasis which in time became important, especially as it coincided with increasingly secular trends in the general climate of opinion. The Act of 1872 had declared that the time or times for any religious observance or instruction must be either at the beginning or at the end, or at the beginning and at the end, of the school meeting. Further, it was stated to be no part of the duties of H.M. Inspectors to inquire into any instruction in religious subjects or to examine any pupil in religious knowledge or in any religious subject or book: and no parliamentary grant might be made in respect of instruction in religious subjects. By these provisions sacred and secular were obviously divided: 'Bible' became a subject confined to a set period in the morning, a subject, moreover, that was not examinable, and therefore likely to be regarded as of secondary importance both by pupils and by teachers, though it is fair to add that school boards made it a practice to invite local ministers to inspect religious instruction. The change might not have been noticeable in the 1870's, but it was ominous for the future.

On the whole it may be said that the Church, though long unable to bear the chief responsibility for public education, had no reason to be ashamed of her proceedings in the three centuries since John Knox sketched his ideal in the *First Book of Discipline*. The total school rolls in 1867 represented one to 6·5 of the population as against one to 6·2 in Prussia where education was compulsory. Nor was the quality of the education to be despised, for at that time, Scotland, with its biblical tradition descending from Knox and with the enlightened ideas of David Stow in recent times, was reckoned to be a generation ahead of England in its educational ideals and practice. As for the effect of the Scottish educational system, some words of Professor

Henry Hamilton in a review of a book on Scottish Chartism may be noted. Referring to why the Scottish Chartists were for the most part 'moral-force' not 'physical-force' men, he says, 'another factor surely was the strong democratic tradition of Scotland, as exemplified in parish school and university and in the Presbyterian form of church government. The Scots had long been accustomed to disputation in which all classes could engage without distinction of birth and status. On the whole, the level of education was such as to make the public amenable to reason and more likely to be influenced by the written word than the fiery oratory of the demagogue.'[37]

10

LATER YEARS AND RETROSPECT

THE inspiration of Chalmers continued to be potent in the social sphere until long past the middle of the nineteenth century, and can be traced in the careers of some of his younger contemporaries, Sheriff Watson, Thomas Guthrie, Norman Macleod, and Hugh Miller.

It was soon found that there were aspects of poverty for which the Poor Law Act of 1845 did not provide. Before that date, indeed, Sheriff Watson of Aberdeen had discovered that there were in that city 280 children under fourteen years of age without any means of subsistence other than begging and stealing. Inspired by a concern for his fellows based on personal religious faith, he began to rouse the public conscience and with the support of a few friends in October 1841 he opened in a small room in Aberdeen an institution for boys which may be regarded as the fountain-head, so far as Scotland is concerned, of ragged schools, industrial schools, and reformatories.[1] The ten children who appeared at the opening were told that they would be given breakfast, dinner, and supper, and would go to their own homes for the night. They would be taught to read and write, and would be given work such as teasing a quantity of hair. The principles of Watson's effort were thus three in number: feed the children; train them in some remunerative employment; and instruct them, especially in a religious sense. Alexander Thomson, the laird of Banchory, one of the Sheriff's chief supporters, described schools of this sort as 'industrial feeding schools'.[2]

During the first few months of the school's existence the average attendance rose from ten to fifty-three, and about one hundred vagrant boys received some benefit, while the superintendent of police attributed to it a decline in thefts by juvenile offenders.[3] In December 1842 a similar institution for girls was opened in Aberdeen.[4] The Sheriff reminded the magistrates that there was a warrant under Act of Parliament for apprehending beggars, and he suggested that they should authorize the police to apprehend children found begging and take them to school. As a result he could write to the Inspector of Prisons, 'We have now no begging children either in town or county. I was rather surprised at the effects produced in the county districts. During the three months preceding 6 July 1843 upwards of a hundred children were found wandering in the county and reported by the rural police. During the corresponding period of 1844 fifty were found. In the corresponding period of 1845 only eight, and from the 8th of June to the 5th of July none were found.'[5] Meantime Watson received numerous requests to speak about his scheme in other places. A school was opened in Dundee in 1842 and in 1846 the Sheriff visited some English cities where a beginning was also made. In Edinburgh both he and the governor of Edinburgh prison made efforts to draw public attention to the problem of juvenile delinquency, and in 1846 Dr. William Robertson, minister of New Greyfriars, established the Vennel Ragged School, described as a 'feeding-school', but it was left to Dr. Thomas Guthrie to rouse the community to a sense of its duty in this matter by the publication in February 1847 of his *Plea For Ragged Schools*.[6]

No one seems to know exactly when ragged schools began. The credit is generally given to John Pounds in England and Thomas Guthrie in Scotland, but Guthrie was anticipated by Sheriff Watson, and a recent writer has said that these schools existed 'long before the writings of Dr. Guthrie of Edinburgh or the school of John Pounds in Portsmouth'. The same authority, however, pays due tribute to both men: 'Yet it was to the inspiration of these two men that the nineteenth century owes many of its Ragged Schools. For about the middle of the century Dr. Guthrie's books on John Pounds and his work were almost best-sellers and many fired by what they had read set out to emulate the example so vividly described.'[7]

Thomas Guthrie (1803–73) came to Edinburgh in 1837 to be minister of the collegiate charge of Old Greyfriars and then in 1840 of St. John's. Under his care were the worst city slums in the Cowgate and Grassmarket, where crime, drunkenness, and squalor ran riot. He joined the Free Church in 1843 but remained in the same district as minister of Free St. John's Church, and there threw himself into the task of grappling with the abundant evils around. Referring to his early Cowgate experiences he said, 'I had not laboured three months in that parish when I became perfectly satisfied of this—that it was impossible to raise the lower classes in towns, unless through the means of the rising generation. In labouring in that district I became also convinced of this—that the only way of reaching the rising generation of the lapsed masses of the community was by such ragged schools.'[8] His conception of a ragged school was that, along with education, both sacred and secular, the children should be furnished gratis with food, clothing, and industrial training. The teaching of a trade, he held, was essential, so that the children might be able eventually to earn their own living and rise above their early environment. His interest was first aroused in ragged schools when at Anstruther in 1841 he saw a picture of John Pounds, the Portsmouth cobbler, in his shop with a group of poor children busy at their lessons around him.[9] The excitements and labours of the Disruption period diverted his attention and kept him so busy that it was not till 1846 that he was free to take action. He first invited his own office-bearers to embark on a scheme in a room in their own church premises, but they feared the responsibility involved and the scheme was abandoned. Then at the beginning of 1847 he appealed in print to the public and met with an immediate and enthusiastic response from citizens of all shades of opinion.[10] He could point out that his scheme united the views of two eminent philanthropists—'Dr. Alison comes in with his bread—Dr. Chalmers with his Bible: here is food for the body—there for the soul'. Soon premises were secured on the Castlehill and a beginning was made. Unfortunately the movement in Edinburgh was soon divided over the question of what form the religious side of the education should take. Guthrie held that he and his Committee had taken the place of parents to the children who came to them, and should therefore give religious instruction in the way they thought right, which meant in a Protestant form, using the Bible in the Authorized Version but no doctrinal catechism. A public meeting of supporters in July 1847 by a large majority took Guthrie's view, but the minority felt constrained to institute another school which they called the United Industrial School. Their complaint was that Guthrie's method practically involved the exclusion of the most necessitous children, those of Roman

Catholic parents; and the plan they adopted was joint secular but separate religious instruction—'to give religious instruction to the children in separate rooms, under teachers of the respective persuasions to which they belonged, and supported by separate funds, altogether apart from the ordinary revenues of the school.'[11]

By the end of 1847 three schools under Guthrie's auspices had been established in Edinburgh, one for boys, one for girls and a third for children of both sexes under ten years of age, the total attendance being 265 children in receipt of food, education and industrial training.[12]

For a description of the environment out of which Ragged School children came one may turn to *Day and Night in the Wynds of Edinburgh* and *Blackfriars' Wynd Analyzed* by a city doctor, George Bell, M.D. He records that in 1850 there were fourteen children belonging to Blackfriars' Wynd in the Original Ragged School, and twice as many more eligible for admission either to it or to analogous schools.[13] How some of those children came to the schools is made clear in one case cited. On 23 March 1850 a policeman came to the Original Ragged School accompanied by a boy of eight and a note from Sheriff Jameson. It appeared that this child, twice previously convicted of theft and twice whipped, had been brought before the court for stealing a waistcoat from a shop-door. The child's father was dead and his mother bore a bad character, and he said he had been taught to steal by an older companion. The Sheriff, however, exercised his power to make the child a witness against a man charged with resetting the waistcoat, and then recommended him to the school.[14] Some indication of the social improvement effected by the schools may be found in the fact that while in 1847 more than five per cent of the prisoners in Edinburgh gaol were under 14— 315 out of 5,734—in 1851 the proportion had fallen to less than one per cent.—56 out of 5,869.[15]

Under Guthrie's eloquent and devoted advocacy the movement spread far and wide in Scotland and beyond. For example, the Glasgow Industrial School Society was instituted in March 1847 and began work in July of that year.[16] In 1849 Guthrie issued a Second Plea for Ragged Schools and in 1859 a Third; while in 1850 an approach was made to the Government and in 1852 a Committee of the House of Commons was appointed, before which he gave evidence. Perhaps at this point an endeavour should be made to distinguish between ragged schools, industrial schools, and reformatories. The last of these, as the name suggests, were from the first associated with crime and consequently with legal and compulsory measures. The other two had originally no association with prisoners and were intended to be voluntary and preventive in character. The first ragged schools were frequently in London and elsewhere merely evening schools where poor children, attending voluntarily and often without the bait of food, got some education. In Guthrie's view, however, both feeding and training for industry were essential; hence ragged schools after his model could also be described as industrial schools. The element of legal compulsion had crept early into Sheriff Watson's schools in Aberdeen, and that same element was partly to be introduced by Act of Parliament into industrial schools, so that the difference between them and reformatories tended to become not so much one of criminality as of age, though industrial schools continued to contain children who had committed no offence, but whose circumstances were such that they were likely to become delinquent.

As a result of the Parliamentary Committee's deliberations two Acts were passed in 1854. One came to be known as Lord Palmerston's Act: it gave power to magistrates to send criminal children under sixteen to a Reformatory School instead of prison. The other, known as Dunlop's Act, was the first Industrial Schools' Act: it applied exclusively to Scotland and it enabled a sheriff or magistrate to commit to an industrial school vagrant children, not exceeding fifteen years of age, even though they were not charged with any offence. Under later Acts of Parliament the classes of children admissible were enlarged to include not only mendicant and destitute children, but those under twelve charged with offences and refractory children under fourteen.[17] By the Elementary Education (Scotland) Act of 1872 the new School Boards were given powers to establish and maintain industrial schools, and, though they were very slow to use these powers, this measure may be regarded as the state's acknowledgment of the value and indeed the necessity of one of the most important social enterprises of the previous generation.

For many years the subject of aid to destitute criminals in

Glasgow had occupied Stevenson Macgill's mind, and towards the end of his life he lent his support to a proposal to erect, by voluntary contributions, a House of Refuge for juvenile delinquents in Glasgow.[18] The outcome was a House of Refuge for boys which was opened in 1838 and one for girls in 1840. The following year an Act of Parliament was secured authorizing the levying of a small assessment on the rental of the city for the upkeep of these institutions. This assessment was the main source of income down to 1854 when Lord Palmerston's Act legalizing Reformatory Schools threw the main burden of support for them on to national funds. As a result institutions like the Glasgow Houses of Refuge increased until by 1864 there were in Scotland twelve Protestant and two Roman Catholic Reformatory Schools containing respectively 724 and 257 children.[19]

One of those who warmly supported Guthrie's efforts was Norman Macleod (1812-72) who was inducted to the Barony parish of Glasgow in July 1851. He had been a student in divinity under Chalmers and, sharing some of the older man's natural characteristics, had come to share also his noble enthusiasms. When he came to Glasgow his parish contained some 87,000 of a population and its numbers were still increasing. There were in it churches belonging to other denominations and, besides his own church, four chapels belonging to the Church of Scotland; but as they had but recently been handed over by the Free Church after a legal decision, they were without ministers and congregations. Even with them, however, the provision was inadequate for the population, especially as it was unevenly distributed. He got six new churches erected in his parish during his ministry, while his missionary staff for dealing with destitute localities increased from one lay missionary employed in 1852 to five missionaries, lay and clerical, with three biblewomen and a colporteur. Although at his coming there were already several day-schools supported by his kirk-session, he found it necessary to raise funds to increase their number, and he also opened evening classes for adults, where grown-up men and women might be found toiling at school tasks from the alphabet upwards. Under the care of his kirk-session there were also seven to twelve Sunday Schools with sometimes as many as fourteen hundred children.

For the social improvement of the parish Macleod founded one of the first congregational Penny Savings Banks in Glasgow, and established a refreshment room where working men could get cheap and well-cooked food and the use of a reading-room at meal hours, instead of having to go to the public houses. The success which crowned these ventures led to the establishment of similar institutions on a larger scale throughout the city.[20] It was said of Chalmers by Lord Rosebery that he 'warmed Glasgow'. The same may with possibly greater emphasis be said of Norman Macleod, and one of the ways in which he did it was by the famous Sunday evening services for the poor, begun in 1857, to which none were admitted unless in their working clothes. The pews were filled with workmen, garbed as on week-days, and women, bare-headed or with an old shawl drawn over their heads. No part of his ministry gave him more interest than this, and the results were notable—many hundreds were reclaimed from lawless habits and a large number became communicants.[21]

Macleod, who was on friendly terms with some of the English Christian Socialists, such as F. D. Maurice, Charles Kingsley, and J. M. Ludlow, was much concerned about the increasing gulf between East-end and West-end. He was dissatisfied, too, with the administration of the Poor Law and paid a visit to Elberfeld to study the system there. One small but not unimportant improvement he proposed and carried through was the complete adoption in Glasgow of the 'boarding-out' system, whereby pauper children were brought up in decent families in the country instead of being herded together in a poorhouse.[22]

Macleod was one of the most sympathetic men who ever lived, and he won a place in the hearts of the poor by his unaffected brotherly attitude towards them individually. He may not have known much about the social sciences, and he may not have realized clearly enough that destitution in cities was an indictment of the social structure as well as an opportunity for the exercise of Christian charity; but he had a big heart and a colossal fund of energy, and his ministry in Glasgow, like that of Chalmers, though not entirely for the same reasons, became something of a legend. In it three things were outstanding: church extension; territorial mission; and the Christian congregation as a society united for work in manifold forms. 'Let congregations,' he declared, 'take cognizance of the whole man and his various earthly relationships, let them seek to enrich him with all Christ gave him, let them endeavour to meet all his wants as an active, social, intellectual, sentient, as well as spiritual being, so that man shall know through the ministrations of the body, the Church, how its living Head gives them all things richly to enjoy!'[23]

Among the disciples of Chalmers a prominent place should be given to Hugh Miller (1802–56), the Cromarty stone-mason who acquired fame as geologist, editor, and author. Like Chalmers he held that economics must be related to the total welfare of man and therefore to ethical and Christian principles. Like Chalmers, too, he was opposed to the principle of legal assessment for poor relief, but he came to the view that it had become inevitable in Scotland since the scheme of Chalmers for a 'thick-set establishment' had not been carried into effect.[24] In particular he could see no other method capable of dealing with the destitution in the Highlands.

When the party in the Church of Scotland which later formed the Free Church started a paper in the interests of their policy at the beginning of 1840, Miller became editor, and from the first showed his social interests. It is indeed noteworthy that he was not so engrossed by the Ten Years' Conflict and the impending Disruption that he neglected to uplift his voice on such issues as the threefold evils of the bothy system, economic, intellectual, and religious,[25] and the deplorable condition of rural housing which called for pecuniary sacrifice on the part of the proprietors.[26] Again in 1844, the year after the Disruption, when ecclesiastical matters might have seemed to demand full space in a Free Church paper, Miller wrote a series of articles warning the people of Scotland against Sir Robert Peel's Scotch Currency Scheme. Miller was suspicious of trades-unions as apt to be tyrannical, and he feared universal or household suffrage, and therefore opposed Chartism.[27] He would, however, have reduced the property qualification for the franchise to as low a figure as £5—a measure which he believed would bring in the respectable working class but exclude the lapsed masses. He was anxious that able-bodied paupers should be set to work, but he was averse to over-much State direction and cherished the ideal of the working classes becoming property-owning.[28] While he gave due publicity and strong support in his paper to social crusades such as those of Sheriff Watson and Dr. Guthrie on behalf of the 'city-Arabs', he opened his columns particularly to James Begg with whose social ideals he had a keen sympathy.

Though the Free Church gave James Begg scope for his social enthusiasms, there were aspects of that Church's social record which evoke less approval. For example, on 5 March 1846 the Free Church Commission of Assembly resolved, without expressing any opinion on the Factory Bills then before Parliament limiting the hours of labour, to address a communication to Lord Ashley setting forth the sense they entertained of the great importance of the service he had rendered to the cause of humanity and the benefit he had thereby conferred on his country.[29] On this Dr. J. R. Fleming justly comments, 'We cannot fail to see here a trace of snobbishness as well as timidity. The Church was ready to compliment a distinguished nobleman, but declined to decide as to the wisdom and rightness of his proposals. She had yet to learn that it was her duty to examine such grievances, and do her utmost for their redress.'[30]

The failure of the Church to give unqualified support to Ashley was partly due to a desire to avoid mere party politics, partly to a reluctance, derived from *laissez-faire* economics, to interfere with the processes of industry and the supposed rights of capital, and partly to the influence of a false spirituality. Of the latter a curious manifestion took place in 1853 in connexion with the outbreak of cholera which during that and the following year caused about six thousand deaths in Scotland, of which 3,892 were in Glasgow and most of the remainder in Edinburgh and Dundee.[31] In October 1853 the Moderator of the Edinburgh Presbytery of the Established Church wrote to Lord Palmerston, then Home Secretary, saying that the Presbytery had considered the propriety of appointing a day of prayer and humiliation within its bounds under the visitation of cholera which had again appeared in the country, but had decided to delay action in order to ascertain whether a national fast was likely to be appointed by the Queen. Palmerston's reply, dated 19 October 1853, was to the effect that he did not think a national fast 'would be suitable to the circumstances of the present moment'. He then proceeded to give the Presbytery a lesson in natural theology, linking sanitation and disease in terms of natural law. 'The Maker of the Universe has established certain laws of nature for the planet in which we live, and the weal or woe of mankind depends upon the observance or neglect of those laws. One of those laws connects health with the absence of those gaseous exhalations which proceed from overcrowded human beings or from decomposing substances, whether animal or vegetable: and those same laws render sickness the almost inevitable consequence of exposure to those noxious influences. But it has at the same time pleased Providence to place it within the power of man to make such arrangements as will prevent or disperse such exhalations as to render them harmless, and it is the duty of man to attend to those laws of nature, and to exert the faculties which Providence has thus given to man for his own welfare. . . . When man has done his utmost for his own safety, then is the time to invoke the blessing of Heaven to give effect to his exertion.'[32]

That, however, was not the last word on the subject, for Palmerston had laid himself open to the retort that as a minister of the Crown he at least bore as much responsibility as the Presbytery for the conditions he had condemned. The Synods of Lothian and Tweeddale of both the Established and Free Churches met on 1 November and appointed Tuesday 29 November as a day of humiliation within their own bounds. In both some decidedly uncomplimentary things were said about the terms of the Home Secretary's letter. In the Established Church Synod Dr. Cook of Haddington, while not defending Palmerston, took up a similar attitude, declaring that 'while he held that it was their duty to humble themselves before God at all times and in all circumstances and to acknowledge that His judgments were just, he thought there was a special call upon them at present to come forward and instruct their ministers to tell those committed to their care of the neglect of those means which God enabled them to see would be effectual for mitigating this disease—that while much had been done for the comfort of the rich, and the improvement of their dwellings, little had been done for the comfort and improvement of the dwellings of the poor—that while they had been widening streets in the wealthier districts of their town, they had been doing so at the expense of the common people, by hemming them into places not fit for human beings to occupy'.[33] It was also pointed out that members of Presbytery had given as much attention as anyone to promoting sanitary measures. In the Free Church Synod James Begg, in supporting a suggestion that there should be introduced into an overture approving of a day of fasting and humiliation some reference to sanitary measures, said: 'they should not neglect the use of physical means. . . . In fact, he thought that those who were admonishing others to look to these were the principal parties who ought to look to these; and it seemed that they were not looking after it as they ought to do, for they were only cleansing the outside of the cup and the platter—whitewashing walls and closes—whilst pestilential masses of filth were festering inside and under foot. They were the parties who ought to look to this, and instead of writing glib letters they ought to do it. This was their proper business; but, on the other hand, it became them, being rulers of a great nation, to acknowledge the hand of Him who was King of nations. . . .'[34]

Begg did not stand alone in Edinburgh at this time in his keen interest in social questions. There was for instance William Garden Blaikie, later a Professor at New College, Edinburgh, whose action was responsible for the formation of the Pilrig Model Dwellings Company. He wrote a successful book for workmen, *Better Days for Working People*, and, being asked to write another for employers, he used his autumn holiday in 1864 to make a tour of English manufacturing towns to get in touch with employers there who had shown a special interest in the welfare of their employees. Earlier that same year he got the Edinburgh Free Church Presbytery to overture the General Assembly on the relation of the Church to social improvement. When the overture came before the Assembly he spoke in its favour but did not press it further, contenting himself with having ventilated the subject. The Assembly approved of the object of the overture, but did not take any action.[35]

It ought not to be forgotten that the social concern of Scottish churchmen was never confined to things which came to expression in Church courts or through the lips of eminent ministers. From the time of Stevenson Macgill and Chalmers onwards there were not lacking men in all the churches who gave themselves to tasks of public philanthropy or rendered notable service in municipal and other public matters under the inspiration of their religious faith. As an example from the sphere of philanthropy one may take William Quarrier, a successful Glasgow

bootmaker and by Christian profession a Baptist, who in 1864
began a shoeblack brigade, and later other brigades, for poor
lads, and in 1871 started a home for destitute children which
soon developed into the Orphan Homes at Bridge of Weir. A
characteristic feature of Quarrier's work was his dependence on
prayer and reports in the press to the exclusion of any canvassing
for subscriptions. In the municipal sphere there was Duncan
McLaren, Lord Provost of Edinburgh from 1851 to 1854 and
later Radical Member of Parliament for the city, mentioned in
connexion with the Forbes Mackenzie Act, whom Dr. J. R.
Fleming described as 'the first man in Scotland to introduce
idealism into municipal affairs'. He added that if he was not free
from 'the one-sidedness and exaggerated individualism that
characterized the Radicalism of the early Victorian era, he had
the sincere conviction and the bold outlook of the genuine reformer'.[36] As a churchman McLaren was a United Presbyterian
of the extreme voluntary type, but he took no part in ecclesiastical
affairs and laboured in the spheres of politics and social reform,
sometimes co-operating with James Begg and sometimes opposing him.

Another example was John Blackie, Lord Provost of Glasgow
from 1863 to 1866, a devoted Free Churchman. Blackie, the son
of the founder of the well-known publishing house, came first
into prominence in Glasgow in 1843 in connexion with three
model lodging-houses then established in the city. During his
term of office as Lord Provost he promoted the City Improvement Scheme which passed through Parliament in 1866. The
scheme dealt with a portion of the old city covering between
fifty and sixty acres, with a population of nearly 60,000. The
trustees were authorized to acquire the property within five
years and to levy assessments to meet the expense of new streets
and other improvements. When the first assessment of sixpence
in the pound was levied the measure became unpopular and
Blackie lost his seat on the Town Council, but the scheme went
on and its great benefits to the sanitary condition of the city were
readily acknowledged.[37]

At this point a tentative conclusion may be ventured to the
effect that as we approach the 1870's the social interest which was
keen during the previous thirty or forty years or longer suffered
a decline. For that we may suggest several reasons. Some of those

12

who had been most actively concerned were now dead, like Chalmers, Collins, Hugh Miller, Brewster, Stow, Dunlop; and others were ending their days in retirement, like George Lewis and Thomas Guthrie; and, while James Begg was still active and zealous for the old causes, his strength was also taken up with more definitely ecclesiastical questions. The paternalism, after the fashion of David Dale and Chalmers, which many men, including Christian industrialists, had carried over from an earlier age, had given place to a more 'business is business' attitude in keeping with the poumant *laissez-faire* economic doctrines. Another reason, which Mr. W. H. Marwick has suggested, is that 'the decline of the mid-century enthusiasm in Church circles as elsewhere' may be attributed 'to the onset of the Great Depression'.[38] The depression is generally dated from 1873 which was 'a year of financial crisis, marking the beginning of the end of an excited spasm of foreign loan making, and initiating a period of falling prices'.[39] This period of falling prices lasted for nearly a quarter of a century, and no doubt business men said and felt that there was a great depression. In fact, however, the term is misleading since the situation then was much less serious than the depression of the inter-war period in the present century. In Scotland, however, the depression was intensified at an early stage by the failure of the City of Glasgow Bank in 1878. Again, there was a feeling abroad that the worst social evils had been removed or were being removed, and that things, now proceeding in the right direction with some momentum, might be left to take their course under the general guidance of Parliament and local authorities. One may take as instance the view expressed in the Free Church Assembly that public attention was now thoroughly alive on the housing question. It was probably easy to take that view when the passing of the second Reform Act in 1867, extending the franchise to the town householder, and so bringing into active citizenship the bulk of the artisan population, seemed to make it certain that enough, if not too much, attention would soon be paid to the desires of the working classes.

Looking back over this survey of ninety years one is bound to confess that social concern was neither so intense nor so widespread among Scottish churchmen as could be wished. In particular, there is a notable lack of official ecclesiastical action regarding the social problems of the early decades of the nineteenth century—the traditional spheres of education and care of the poor always excepted. The Highland clearances were not seriously challenged and the sores of slumdom—poverty, disease, vice, and crime—festered while the church courts were too long silent. Yet social concern was never altogether lacking, and it must be stressed that the early Victorian period, say 1840 to 1865, showed much more of it than is commonly believed. It is true that if one equates social concern with enthusiasm for Socialism or even for the Welfare State, then one will find little of it in the Church, or indeed anywhere else, in Victorian times. But then, in such an equation, is not a big question being begged? Is it not possible that as true a social concern, and possibly even a wiser and more Christian social concern, was manifest, in James Begg's ideal of working men owning their own houses and gardens and of large estates being transformed into small family farms of some fifty acres, than in the centralized socialistic ideal of the state as the almost universal property-owner? There is some support in history for the view that the distribution of political power in a state, whatever its nominal constitution, is in fact dependent on the distribution of property, and that only a society marked by widely-distributed property rights can be truly free. At all events, zealous prosecution of the latter ideal has as much right as socialist agitation to be called social concern. Moreover, one must not fail to salute with admiration and gratitude that social concern or active compassion which may seldom express its mind on the more public aspects of social affairs, but which has been an ever-present element in much that we have surveyed. Thus one may conclude by agreeing with a contemporary historian that 'whatever mistakes Christians may make about mundane problems or by way of prudential calculation, still they are always right in so far as they teach and exemplify Christian charity'.[40]

REFERENCES

Introduction

1 *English Historical Review*, LXIV, p. 377.
2 Thomas Thomson, ed., *The Booke of the Universall Kirk of Scotland*, iii, p. 874.
3 *General Assembly Commission Records 1648–9* (Scottish History Society 1896), p. 86.
4 Archibald Bruce, *True Patriotism*, 1785, p. 17.
5 ibid., pp. 97 f.

Chapter 1: The Agrarian and Industrial Revolutions

1 H. Hamilton, *Scottish Historical Review*, XXV, p. 191.
2 *The Old Statistical Account* [hereafter referred to as *OSA*], vol. 20, p. 6 (Livingstone); 11, p. 263 (Wattin); 20, pp. 474 f. (Dowally).
3 *OSA* 2, p. 162 (Neilston).
4 *OSA* 10, p. 341 (Carnwath); *The New Statistical Account* [hereafter referred to as *NSA*] 6, p. 404 (Cadder); *NSA* 6, p. 339 (Crawford); *NSA* 7, p. 511 (Cathcart).
5 A. R. B. Haldane, *The Drove Roads of Scotland*, ch. 11 and appendix map; M. Gray, *The Highland Economy, 1750–1850*, pp. 37 f.
6 *OSA* 11, p. 593 (Callander); *OSA* 5, pp. 472 f. (Inverchaolain); *OSA* 3, pp. 184 f. (Lochgoilhead and Kilmorich).
7 *OSA* 20, p. 2 (Livingstone); *OSA* 7, p. 602 (Muirkirk); *OSA* 2, p. 78 (Galston); *OSA* 5, p. 325 (Currie); *OSA* 2, p. 162 (Neilston).
8 *OSA* 20, pp. 152 f. (Sorn).
9 J. U. Nef, *Rise of the British Coal Industry*, i, p. 43.
10 *OSA* 7, p. 11 (Stevenston); *OSA* 11, p. 492 (Carnock); *OSA* 5, p. 533 (Glasgow); *OSA* 5, p. 257 (Cambuslang); *OSA* 9, p. 8 (Rutherglen).
11 *OSA* 2, p. 368 (Ecclesmachan); *OSA* 3, p. 464 (Dalziel); *OSA* 9, p. 337 (St. Monance); *OSA* 4, p. 329 (Aberdour).
12 *OSA* 5, p. 346 (Cathcart); *OSA* 7, p. 402 (Oldhamstocks); *OSA* 1, p. 373 (Kettle); *OSA* 12, p. 102 (Dalry).
13 J. M. Dickie, *Scottish Historical Review*, XVIII, p. 19.
14 *OSA* 11, p. 271 (Wattin); *OSA* 11, p. 604 (Callander); *OSA* 7, p. 208 (Nigg); *OSA* 7, p. 252 (Urray).
15 G. M. Mitchell, *Scottish Historical Review*, XXII, p. 102.
16 *OSA* 10, p. 422 and *OSA* 1, pp. 304 f.
17 *OSA* 5, pp. 258 f. (Cambuslang).
18 W. H. Marwick, *Scottish Historical Review*, XXI, p. 213.
19 *NSA* 5, p. 503 (Kirkmichael); *NSA* 5, p. 371 (Maybole).
20 *OSA* 8, p. 302 (Kelton); *OSA* 11, pp. 56 f. (Rerrick).
21 G. M. Mitchell, *Scottish Historical Review*, XXII, p. 102.
22 *NSA* 7, p. 326 (Neilston); *NSA* 6, pp. 145 and 153 (Glasgow).
23 G. M. Mitchell, *Scottish Historical Review*, XXII, p. 103.
24 *OSA* 15, p. 40 (Lanark).

25 R. Owen, *A New View of Society*, 4th ed., 1818, p. 37.
26 *OSA* 15, p. 40 (Lanark).
27 *OSA* 20, p. 181 (Sorn).
28 *OSA* 12, p. 116 (Barony of Glasgow).
29 *NSA* 6, p. 322 (Blantyre).
30 *OSA* 13, p. 479 (Dunfermline).
31 R. Owen, *Life of Robert Owen* by himself, vol. 1, 1857, p. 60.
32 *OSA* 15, p. 35 f. (Lanark).
33 R. Owen, *A New View of Society*, 4th ed. 1818, pp. 36 f.
34 R. Owen, *Address to the Inhabitants of New Lanark* (1816).
35 R. Owen, *A New View of Society*, 4th ed. 1818, pp. 38 f.
36 *OSA*, 11, p. 132 (Kilmore and Kilbride).
37 *OSA* 12, p. 114 (Barony of Glasgow).
38 *NSA* 6, p. 322 (Blantyre).
39 *OSA* 8, p. 302 and *NSA* 4, p. 168 (Kelton).
40 T. Thomson, *Biographical Dictionary of Eminent Scotsmen*, 1856, vol. V,
    p. 176.
41 J. O. Mitchell, *Old Glasgow Essays*, pp. 41 f.
42 T. Thomson, op. cit., V, p. 173.
43 ibid. V, 173.
44 J. Ross, *History of Congregational Independency in Scotland*, p. 39.
45 T. Thomson, op. cit. V, p. 175.
46 *Substance of a Discourse by David Dale, Esq.*, pp. 4–7.
47 T. Thomson, op. cit. V, pp. 175 f.
48 G. Struthers, *History of the Relief Church*, p. 183.
49 T. Thomson, op. cit. V, pp. 174 f.
50 *OSA* 20, p. 176 (Sorn).
51 *OSA* 20, pp. 88 f. (Kilmadock).
52 *OSA* 3, p. 185 (Lochgoilhead and Kilmorich) cf. *OSA* 10, p. 340 (Carn-
    wath) and *OSA* 16, p. 193 (Assint).
53 *OSA* 8, p. 374 (Criech); *OSA* 3, p. 543 (Farr); *OSA* 9, p. 31 (Golspie).
54 *OSA* 11, p. 56 (Rerrick); *OSA* 20, p. 176 (Sorn); *OSA* 17, pp. 531 f.
    (Balfron).
55 *OSA* 7, p. 390 (Old Monkland).
56 *OSA* 11, p. 56 (Rerrick), cf. *OSA* 5, p. 325 (Currie).
57 *OSA* 19, p. 86 (Falkirk); *OSA* 15, p. 495 (Kilbarchan); *OSA* 5, p. 534
    (Glasgow).
58 *OSA* 20, pp. 183 f. (Sorn).
59 *NSA* 9, p. 123 (Leslie), cf. *NSA* 11, p. 231 (Kinnettles).
60 *NSA* 6, p. 313 (Avondale), cf. *NSA* 5, pp. 53 f. (Ayr).
61 *NSA* 8, p. 81 (Row).
62 *OSA* 8, p. 19 (Dornoch).
63 *NSA* 7, p. 270 (Paisley).
64 *OSA* 8, p. 238 (Dundee); *NSA* 6, p. 324 (Blantyre); *NSA* 6, p. 634 (Shotts);
    NSA 9, p. 313 (Cameron).
65 *OSA* 2, p. 163 and *NSA* 7, p. 332 (Neilston). For a similar proposal see
    G. Lewis, *The State of St. David's Parish*, Dundee, 1841, p. 9.
66 *NSA* 8, p. 165 (Kilsyth).
67 *NSA* 8, pp. 294 f. (Balfron).
68 *NSA* 6, pp. 697 f. (Govan), cf. *OSA* 15, p. 38 (Lanark).
69 *NSA* 5, p. 371 (Maybole).
70 *NSA* 5, p. 233 (Dalry); *NSA* 6, p. 298 (Glasford).
71 *OSA* 2, p. 163 (Neilston).
72 *NSA* 11, p. 225 (Kinnettles).
73 *NSA* 6, p. 697 f. (Govan).
74 *OSA* 20, p. 177 (Sorn); *NSA* 8, p. 294 (Balfron); *NSA* 5, p. 233 (Dalry).
75 *NSA* 9, pp. 119 f. (Leslie).
76 *NSA* 8, p. 366 (Larbert).
77 *NSA* 8, p. 237 (Campsie).
78 *NSA* 6, p. 324 (Blantyre).

79 *NSA* 8, p. 237 (Campsie).
80 *NSA* 9, p. 253 (Auchtertool) cf. *NSA* 7, p. 252 (Paisley).
81 *NSA* 8, p. 294 (Balfron).
82 *NSA* 5, p. 319 (Dalmellington).
83 *OSA* 5, pp. 340 f. (Cathcart).
84 *NSA* 7, p. 508 (Cathcart).
85 *NSA* 5, pp. 371 f. (Maybole).
86 *NSA* 8, p. 168 (Kilsyth).
87 *NSA* 11, p. 225 (Kinnettles).
88 *NSA* 11, pp. 29 and 53 (Dundee).
89 *NSA* 11, pp. 517 f. (St. Vigeans).
90 *NSA* 7, p. 437 (Greenock).
91 *NSA* 5, pp. 668 f. (Dundonald).
92 *OSA* 5, p. 535 (Glasgow).
93 *NSA* 8, p. 37 (Falkirk).
94 *OSA* 20, pp. 87 f. (Kilmadock).
95 *Report from the Poor Law Commissioners on an Inquiry into the Sanitary Condition of the Labouring Population*, 1842, p. 122.
96 M. Gray, 'Economic Welfare and Money Income in the Highlands 1750–1850', in *Scottish Journal of Political Economy*, vol. 2, pp. 57–63.
97 A. Pope, *Essay on Man*, Ep. IV.
98 Charles Wilson, 'The Entrepreneur in the Industrial Revolution in Britain,' in *History*, vol. XLII, No. 145, June, 1957, p. 114.

Chapter 2 : Progress and Poverty

1 J. H. F. Brotherston, *Observations on the Early Public Health Movement in Scotland*, 1952, p. 2.
2 ibid., pp. 26–33.
3 ibid., p. 34.
4 ibid., pp. 43–47.
5 R. Graham, M.D., *Practical Observations on Continued Fever*, 1818, p. 64.
6 R. Perry, M.D., *Facts and Observations on the Sanatory* [sic] *State of Glasgow*, 1844, p. 7.
7 G. Lewis, *The State of St. David's Parish*, Dundee, 1841, pp. 13 f.
8 R. Cowan, M.D., *Vital Statistics of Glasgow*, 1840, p. 5.
9 Rait and Pryde, *Scotland*, 2nd ed., 1954, p. 238 and D. F. Macdonald, *Scotland's Shifting Population*, p. 84.
10 R. Cowan, M.D., op. cit., p. 34.
11 *Reports on the Sanitary Condition of the Labouring Population of Scotland*, 1842, p. 162.
12 ibid., pp. 165 f.
13 J. Smith, *The Grievances of the Working Classes, and the Pauperism and Crime of Glasgow with their Causes, Extent and Remedies*, 1846, p. 9.
14 ibid., p. 101.
15 ibid., p. 33.
16 R. Cowan, M.D., op. cit., p. 34.
17 J. Smith, op. cit., p. 27.
18 George Bell, M.D., *Day and Night in the Wynds of Edinburgh*, 3rd ed. 1849, p. 10.
19 *Reports on the Sanitary Condition of the Labouring Population of Scotland*, 1842, pp. 210 f.
20 ibid., p. 221.
21 ibid., p. 263.
22 ibid., pp. 250 f.
23 R. Cowan, M.D., op. cit., p. 33.
24 Charles Creighton, *History of Epidemics in Britain*, 1894, II, p. 190.
25 ibid., II, p. 204.
26 R. Cowan, M.D., op. cit., p. 33.

27 ibid., p. 33.
28 *Reports on the Sanitary Condition of the Labouring Population of Scotland,* 1842, p. 77.
29 R. Cowan, M.D., op. cit., pp. 35 f.
30 T. Ferguson, *The Dawn of Scottish Social Welfare,* 1944, pp. 147 f., and J. H. F. Brotherston, op. cit., p. 100.

Chapter 3: Pioneers in Country and City

1 T. Thomson, *Biographical Dictionary of Eminent Scotsmen,* 1856, V, pp. 201 f.
2 G. J. C. Duncan, *Memoir of Rev. Henry Duncan, D.D. of Ruthwell,* pp. 51–7, and S. Hall, *Dr. Duncan of Ruthwell,* pp. 42 f.
3 *Dictionary of National Biography,* and *The Centenary of Savings Banks* (Memorial Volume), 1910, p. 10.
4 T. Thomson, op. cit., p. 203.
5 Henry Duncan, *An Essay on the Nature and Advantages of Parish Banks,* 1815, pp. 8 f.
6 ibid., p. 10.
7 *Third Report from Select Committee on Poor Laws, with Appendix containing returns from the General Assembly,* 1818, p. 37.
8 Henry Duncan, op. cit., p. 21.
9 D. K. and C. J. Guthrie, *Memoirs of Thomas Guthrie,* I, p. 422.
10 ibid., pp. 108 f.
11 Robert Burns, *Memoir of the Rev. Stevenson Macgill, D.D.,* 1842, p. 25.
12 ibid., p. 43.
13 ibid., p. 47.
14 T. Thomson, op. cit., V, p. 410.
15 R. Burns, op. cit., p. 46.
16 James Cleland, *Statistical Tables relative to the City of Glasgow,* 3rd ed. 1823, p. 95.
17 S. Macgill, *Discourses and Essays on Subjects of Public Interest,* 1819, p. 171.
18 S. Macgill, *On Lunatic Asylums,* 1810.
19 T. Ferguson, *The Dawn of Scottish Social Welfare,* 1948, pp. 276 f.
20 S. Macgill, *Discourses and Essays, etc.,* 1819, p. 137.
21 ibid., pp. 144–52.
22 ibid., p. 473.
23 ibid., pp. 471–5.
24 *Abridgement of the Acts and Proceedings of the General Assembly,* 1819, p. 43.
25 R. Burns, op. cit., pp. 49 f.
26 ibid., pp. 50–53; *Abridgement of the Act and Proceedings, etc.,* 1820, p. 45; 1823, p. 53.
27 H. M. B. Reid, *The Divinity Professors in the University of Glasgow,* 1923, p. 288.
28 John Dunlop, *Autobiography,* p. 7.
29 R. Burns, op. cit., pp. 18 and 334; D. Keir, *The House of Collins,* p. 23.
30 T. Smith, *Memoirs of James Begg, D.D.,* 1885, i, p. 141.

Chapter 4: The Social Policy of Thomas Chalmers

1 T. Chalmers, *Select Works,* IX, p. 459.
2 ibid., IX, p. 241.
3 ibid., IX, p. 257.
4 ibid., X, p. 687.
5 ibid., X, p. 342.
6 ibid., IX, pp. 395 f.
7 ibid., X, p. 5.
8 ibid., IX, p. 473.
9 ibid., IX, p. 246.

10 W. Hanna, *Memoirs of the Life and Writings of Thomas Chalmers*, ii, p. 264.
11 See an account of this experiment in his *Polity of a Nation* (*Select Works*, X, ch. xii, also appendices); also W. Hanna, op. cit., ii, ch. xiii.
12 See letter to Campbell Nasmyth in W. Hanna, op. cit., ii, pp. 300 f.
13 T. Chalmers, *Select Works*, X, pp. 654 f.
14 ibid., X, p. 715: also W. Hanna, op. cit., ii, p. 314.
15 T. Chalmers, *On the Sufficiency of the Parochial System without a Poor Rate, etc.*, *Works*, XXI, p. 175.
16 W. Hanna, op. cit., iii, p. 21.
17 D. K. and C. J. Guthrie, *Memoirs of Thomas Guthrie*, I, p. 422.
18 W. Hanna, op. cit., ii, p. 121.
19 T. Chalmers, *Select Works*, X, pp. 492 ff.
20 ibid., IX, pp. 40 and 58; X, pp. 510 f.
21 ibid., X, p. 494.
22 ibid., IX, pp. 278 f.
23 W. P. Alison, *Observations on the Management of the Poor in Scotland*, 1840, p. 73.
24 J. S. Davy, in *Reports on the Elberfeld Poor-Law System presented to Parliament*, 1888, p. 10.
25 A. F. Young and E. T. Ashton, *British Social Work in the Nineteenth Century*, 1956, p. 80.
26 ibid., p. 97.
27 ibid., p. 113.
28 ibid., p. 78.
29 John A. Mack in *The Glasgow Herald*, 4 May 1957.

Chapter 5: The Scottish Church and the Poor

1 *APS*, ii, 251, c. 14.
2 *First Book of Discipline*, V, 6.
3 *APS*, iii, 86–88.
4 *APS*, viii, 89–91.
5 *Report of Poor Law Commissioners* (Scotland), 1909, p. 310.
6 D. F. Macdonald, *Scotland's Shifting Population*, p. 113.
7 *Report of Committee of General Assembly*, 1818, p. 36, being Appendix to *Third Report of Select Committee on Poor Laws*.
8 ibid., p. 25.
9 *Report of Poor Law Commissioners* (Scotland), 1909, p. 312.
10 *Report of Committee of General Assembly*, 1818, p. 35.
11 *Report of Poor Law Commissioners* (Scotland), 1909, p. 312.
12 *First Book of Discipline*, V, 6.
13 J. M. McPherson, *The Kirk's Care of the Poor*, pp. 117 f.
14 ibid., pp. 135 f.
15 ibid., p. 149.
16 *OSA*, 2, p. 112.
17 S. Macgill, *Discourses and Essays*, p. 466.
18 A. Alison, *The Principles of Population*, II, p. 232.
19 G. Lewis, *The State of St. David's Parish*, Dundee, pp. 27 f.
20 S. Macgill, op. cit., p. 442.
21 ibid., p. 475.
22 *Edinburgh Christian Instructor*, vol. XIX, 1820, pp. 805 f.
23 T. Chalmers, *Works*, XIV, p. 401.
24 ibid., p. 372.
25 W. P. Alison, *Observations on the Management of the Poor in Scotland*, 2nd ed., 1840, p. x.
26 ibid., p. v.
27 W. P. Alison, *Reply to Dr. Chalmers' Objections*, 1841, p. 55.
28 ibid., p. 8.
29 W. P. Alison, *Observations etc.*, 2nd ed., pp. 75–84.

30 ibid., pp. 105–10.
31 A. Alison, op. cit., II, pp. 224 f.
32 ibid., p. 228.
33 ibid., pp. 186 f.
34 ibid., pp. 233 f.
35 P. Brewster, *Chartist and Military Discourses*, pp. 97 f.
36 T. Carlyle, *Past and Present*. Part I, ch. i.
37 *OSA*, 15, p. 641.
38 *OSA*, 8, p. 19.
39 R. Burns, *Historical Dissertation on the Law and Practice of Great Britain, and particularly of Scotland with regard to the poor*, 2nd ed. 1819, p. 274.
40 *Report of the Lords Committee on the Poor Law*, 1817, Appendix, p. 55.
41 *Report of Committee of General Assembly*, 1818, being Appendix to *Third Report of Select Committee on Poor Laws*, p. 31.
42 R. Burns, *A Plea for the Poor of Scotland*, p. 7, quoted L. J. Saunders, *Scottish Democracy*, p. 411.
43 *Proceedings of General Assembly*, 1841, pp. 34–59 and 323–5.
44 J. H. F. Brotherston, *Observations on the Early Public Health Movement in Scotland*, p. 75.
45 *Third Report from Select Committee on the Poor Laws*, 1818, p. 26.

Chapter 6: *John Dunlop and the Scottish Temperance Reformation*

1 *Minutes of Evidence before the Select Committee*, 1834, p. 176.
2 ibid., pp. 530 f.
3 G. Lewis, *State of St. David's Parish*, Dundee, p. 33.
4 *OSA*, 13, pp. 438 f.
5 *OSA*, 17, p. 536.
6 *OSA*, 10, p. 98.
7 *OSA*, 10, pp. 71 f.
8 *Minutes of Evidence, etc.*, p. 177.
9 M. B. Macgregor, *Towards Scotland's Social Good*, p. 19.
10 L. J. Saunders, *Scottish Democracy 1815–40*, p. 232.
11 *Minutes of Evidence, etc.*, p. 323.
12 ibid., p. 533.
13 ibid, pp. 175 f.
14 G. Lewis, op. cit., pp. 14–20.
15 T. Ferguson, *Dawn of Scottish Social Welfare*, p. 27.
16 A. Alison, *Principles of Population*, II, p. 80.
17 *Works of Thomas Reid*, 1849, p. 40.
18 *NSA*, 6, p. 718.
19 A. Alison, op. cit., II, pp. 113 f.
20 P. T. Winskill, *The Temperance Movement and Its Workers*, 1891, I, p. 31.
21 ibid., I, p. 80.
22 W. Logan, *Early Heroes of The Temperance Reformation*, pp. 29 f.
23 D. Keir, *The House of Collins*, p. 94.
24 *Minutes of Evidence, etc.*, p. 511.
25 W. Logan, op. cit., p. 61.
26 P. T. Winskill, op. cit., I, p. 58.
27 J. Dunlop, *Artificial Drinking Usages of North Britain*, 4th ed. 1836, p. 6.
28 *Minutes of Evidence, etc.*, p. 531.
29 J. Dunlop, *On the Wine System of Great Britain*, 1831, pp. 40 ff.
30 J. Dunlop, *Artificial Drinking Usages of North Britain*, 4th ed., 1836, p. 79.
31 *Minutes of Evidence, etc.*, p. 523.
32 J. Dunlop, *On the Wine System of Great Britain*, p. 43.
33 *Minutes of Evidence, etc.*, p. 522.
34 J. Dunlop, *Artificial Drinking Usages of North Britain*, 4th ed., p. 24.
35 ibid., p. 102.
36 P. T. Winskill, op. cit., I, p. 72.

37 ibid., I, p. 59.
38 ibid., I, p. 80.
39 W. Logan, op. cit., p. 82.
40 *Autobiography of John Dunlop*, p. 91.
41 E. Morris, *History of the Temperance and Teetotal Societies of Glasgow*, 1855, p. 15.
42 ibid., p. 55.
43 ibid., p. 212.
44 ibid., p. 62.
45 D. Keir, op. cit., pp. 106 f.
46 *Autobiography of John Dunlop*, p. 93.
47 ibid., pp. 109 f.
48 ibid., p. 120 note.
49 E. Morris, op. cit., p. 85.
50 ibid., p. 92.
51 ibid., pp. 96–104.
52 D. Keir, op. cit., p. 206.
53 *Autobiography of John Dunlop*, p. 115.
54 ibid., p. 168.
55 ibid., pp. 394 f.
56 ibid., p. 428.
57 *Memoir of Rev. William Arnot*, pp. 250–5.
58 M. B. Macgregor, op. cit., p. 37.
59 D. Jamie, *John Hope*, 1907, pp. 70–81.
60 ibid., p. 49.
61 *Minutes of Evidence, etc.*, p. 190.
62 *Transactions of National Association for Promotion of Social Science*, 1874, pp. 922 f.
63 J. B. Mackie, *Life and Work of Duncan McLaren*, I, p. 306.
64 *Minutes of Evidence, etc.*, p. 188.
65 E. Morris, op. cit., p. 156.
66 J. B. Mackie, op. cit., I, p. 309.
67 *Minutes of Evidence, etc.*, pp. 535 f.
68 ibid., p. 328.
69 E. Morris, op. cit., pp. 68 and 74.
70 P. T. Winskill, op. cit., I, p. 82 and W. Logan, op. cit., pp. 64–68.
71 J. R. Fleming, *The Church in Scotland, 1843–1874*, p. 77.

Chapter 7 : Patrick Brewster and Scottish Chartism

1 L. C. Wright, *Scottish Chartism*, 1953.
2 *The Chartist Circular*, 28 March 1840, p. 110.
3 *The Chartist Circular*, 2 May 1840, pp. 129 f.
4 L. C. Wright, op. cit., p. 104.
5 ibid., p. 104.
6 W. H. Marwick, *Economic Developments in Victorian Scotland*, p. 125.
7 T. Ferguson, *The Dawn of Scottish Social Welfare*, pp. 189 f.
8 C. Stewart Black, *The Story of Paisley*, pp. 187–90.
9 R. Brown, *History of Paisley*, II, pp. 276–86.
10 ibid., I, pp. 102 f.
11 *MS. Minutes of the Presbytery of Paisley.*
12 R. Brown, op. cit., I, pp. 103 f.
13 *MS. Minutes of the Presbytery of Paisley.*
14 *Proceedings of the General Assembly of the Church of Scotland*, 1842, pp. 292–5.
15 *The Witness*, 4 June 1842.
16 *Proceedings of the General Assembly of the Church of Scotland*, 1842, p. 297.
17 *The Scottish Guardian*, 7 June 1842.
18 P. Brewster, *The Seven Chartist and Military Discourses*, 1843, p. 421.

19 *The Principal Acts of the General Assembly of the Church of Scotland, etc.*, 1843, p. 65.
20 R. Brown, op. cit., I, p. 105.
21 *The Principal Acts of the General Assembly of the Church of Scotland, etc.*, 1843, p. 51.
22 P. Brewster, op. cit., pp. 422 f.
23 ibid., p. 424.
24 ibid., pp. 63 f.
25 ibid., pp. 99 f.
26 ibid., p. 103.
27 ibid., p. 122.
28 ibid., p. 128.
29 ibid., p. 417.
30 ibid., pp. 419 f.
31 *Press-cutting in Brewster's Scrap-book*, p. 32.
32 ibid., p. 14.
33 ibid., p. 62.
34 P. Brewster, op. cit., p. 95.
35 ibid., p. 116.
36 *The Glasgow Courier*, 27 Apr. 1848.
37 M. M. Gordon, *The Home Life of Sir David Brewster*, p. 42.

Chapter 8: *James Begg and the Housing of the Working Classes*

1 T. Smith, *Memoirs of James Begg*, i, p. 141.
2 *Proceedings of the General Assembly of the Free Church of Scotland*, 1850, p. 217.
3 J. Begg, *Happy Homes for Working Men*, p. iii.
4 *The Witness*, 17 Jan. 1849.
5 ibid., 12 Jan. 1850.
6 J. Begg., op. cit., p. 153.
7 ibid., p. 9.
8 *Transactions of National Social Science Association*, 1858, p. 622.
9 J. Begg, op. cit., p. 14.
10 *Reports on the Sanitary Condition of the Labouring Population of Scotland*, 1842, pp. 154 f.
11 Quoted, ibid, p. 71.
12 *Report from Poor Law Commissioners on an Inquiry into the Sanitary Condition of the Labouring Population*, 1842, pp. 23 ff.
13 ibid., p. 121.
14 ibid., p. 122.
15 ibid., p. 141.
16 W. G. Blaikie, *An Autobiography*, pp. 156–9.
17 J. Begg, op. cit., pp. 14 f.
18 ibid., p. 124.
19 ibid., p. 19.
20 *The Witness*, 23 Jan. 1858.
21 *The Scotsman*, 19 Oct. 1858.
22 *Transactions of National Social Science Association*, 1863, p. 764.
23 *Proceedings of General Assembly of the Free Church of Scotland*, 1858, pp. 237 f.
24 *Proceedings of the General Assembly of the Free Church of Scotland*, 1859, p. 57.
25 *Transactions of National Social Science Association*, 1858, p. 623.
26 *Proceedings of the General Assembly of the Free Church of Scotland*, 1861, p. 326.
27 *Report of Committee on Housing of the Working Classes*, 1862, p. 8.
28 ibid., pp. 14 f.

29 *Proceedings of the General Assembly of the Free Church of Scotland*, 1862, pp. 192, 341, 372.
30 *Report of Committee on Housing of the Working Classes*, 1866, p. 3.
31 ibid., 1867, pp. 6 f.
32 ibid., p. 5.
33 *Proceedings of the General Assembly of the Free Church of Scotland*, 1867, p. 485.
34 J. Begg, op. cit., pp. 28–35.
35 *Transactions of National Social Science Association*, 1863, p. 629.
36 J. Begg, op. cit., pp. 48–56.
37 *The Watchword*, 1 Sept. 1866.
38 *Transactions of National Social Science Association*, 1874, pp. 908 f.
39 ibid., pp. 913 f.
40 *Report of Royal Commission on the Housing of the Industrial Population of Scotland*, 1918, p. 267.
41 ibid., p. 266.
42 *Transactions of National Social Science Association*, 1860, pp. 783 ff.
43 J. Begg, op. cit., p. iv.
44 ibid., pp. 61–63.
45 *The Witness*, 6 Jan. 1847.
46 T. Smith, *Memoirs of James Begg*, ii, 188 f.
47 *Proceedings of the General Assembly of the Free Church of Scotland*, 1859, pp. 288–91.

Chapter 9: The Scottish Church and Education

1 *Autobiography and Diary of James Melvill* (Wodrow Society), pp. 16 f.
2 T. McCrie, *Life of Andrew Melville*, 1856, p. 471 Note on Parochial Schools.
3 A. Edgar, *Old Church Life in Scotland*, 2nd Series, p. 75.
4 *A Short Account of the Rise, Progress and Present State of the Society in Scotland for Propagating Christian Knowledge*, 1748.
5 *Records of the Scottish Church History Society*, III, p. 194.
6 Rait and Pryde, *Scotland* (1954 edition), p. 292.
7 G. Lewis, *Scotland a Half-Educated Nation*, p. 19.
8 *Appendix to Report of Select Committee on the Poor Laws*, 1818, p. 40.
9 R. K. Webb, 'Literacy among the Working Classes in Nineteenth Century Scotland', *Scottish Historical Review*, XXXIII, pp. 102–6.
10 D. Macmillan, *Life of Robert Flint*, pp. 4 f.
11 G. Pratt Insh, *Life and Work of David Stow*, 1938, p. 6.
12 W. Fraser, *Memoir of the Life of David Stow*, 1868, p. 20.
13 W. Hanna, *Life of Thomas Chalmers*, ii, p. 122.
14 W. Fraser, op. cit., p. 41.
15 ibid., p. 65.
16 ibid., pp. 70–73.
17 ibid., p. 83.
18 ibid., pp. 117–26.
19 ibid., p. 127.
20 G. Lewis, *Scotland a Half-Educated Nation*, p. 22.
21 ibid., p. 73.
22 ibid., p. 65.
23 ibid., p. 44.
24 ibid., p. 75.
25 W. Fraser, op. cit., pp. 166, 171.
26 N. Walker, *Chapters from the History of the Free Church of Scotland*, p. 119.
27 W. Fraser, op. cit., pp. 186–201.
28 *2nd Report by H.M. Commissioners appointed to inquire into the Schools of Scotland*, 1867, p. xix.
29 ibid., p. lv.
30 ibid., p. clxxiv.

31 ibid., p. xxxviii.
32 ibid., p. xx.
33 ibid., p. xliv.
34 A. Gordon, *Life of A. H. Charteris*, p. 146.
35 *Memorandum on Religious Instruction in the Schools in Scotland*, 1943, p. 5.
36 *Report of Scottish Education Department, 1878–79*, p. 173.
37 *Scottish Historical Review*, XXXIII, pp. 68 f.

Chapter 10: Later Years and Retrospect

1 H. F. Henderson, *Religion in Scotland*, 1920, p. 188.
2 G. Smeaton, *Memoir of Alexander Thomson of Banchory*, 1869, pp. 181, 332–40, 345 f.
3 *The Witness*, 23 July 1842.
4 ibid., 4 Mar. 1843.
5 ibid., 24 Feb. 1847.
6 H. Scott, *Fasti Ecclesiae Scoticanae*, I, p. 36 and D. K. and C. J. Guthrie, *Memoirs of Thomas Guthrie, D.D.*, II, pp. 114 and 119.
7 A. F. Young and E. T. Ashton, *British Social Work in the Nineteenth Century*, 1956, p. 240.
8 D. K. and C. J. Guthrie, op. cit., I, p. 378.
9 ibid., II, pp. 112 f.
10 ibid., II, pp. 116–20.
11 Alex. Nicolson, *Memoirs of Adam Black*, pp. 143 f.
12 D. K. and C. J. Guthrie, op. cit., II, p. 132.
13 George Bell, M.D., *Blackfriars' Wynd Analyzed*, 1850, p. 14.
14 ibid., p. 25 f.
15 D. K. and C. J. Guthrie, op. cit., II, p. 136.
16 William Logan, *Moral Statistics of Glasgow*, 1849, p. 52.
17 *Memorandum on the Reformatory and Industrial Schools of Great Britain.* H.M. Stationery Office, 1904, pp. 10 f.
18 R. Burns, *Memoir of the Rev. Stevenson Macgill, D.D.*, 1842, p. 301 f.
19 J. Rae, *Reformatories*, 1867, pp. 15–18.
20 Donald Macleod, *Memoir of Norman Macleod, D.D.*, 1891, pp. 231–3.
21 ibid., pp. 261–4.
22 ibid., p. 241.
23 ibid., p. 229.
24 *The Witness*, 15 Feb. 1843.
25 ibid., 8 Sept. 1841 and 22 Sept. 1841.
26 ibid., 22 Jan. 1842.
27 ibid., 7 June 1848 and 26 Sept. 1840.
28 ibid., 17 June 1854.
29 ibid., 7 Mar. 1846.
30 J. R. Fleming, *The Church in Scotland, 1843–1874*, p. 99.
31 T. Ferguson, *The Dawn of Scottish Social Welfare*, p. 129.
32 *The Witness*, 29 Oct. 1853.
33 ibid., 2 Nov. 1853.
34 ibid., 2 Nov. 1853.
35 *Proceedings of the General Assembly of the Free Church of Scotland*, 1864, pp. 324 ff.
36 J. R. Fleming, op. cit., p. 153.
37 *Biographical Sketches of the Lord Provosts of Glasgow, 1833–1883*, pp. 237–40 and 298.
38 W. H. Marwick, *Economic Developments in Victorian Scotland*, p. 176.
39 H. L. Beales, 'The "Great Depression" in Industry and Trade', *Economic History Review*, V.
40 Herbert Butterfield, *Christianity in European History*, p. 56.

INDEX

PRINTED IN GREAT BRITAIN
BY EBENEZER BAYLIS AND SON, LIMITED, THE
TRINITY PRESS, WORCESTER, AND LONDON